History Quest: Early Times
Study Guide

by Lisa Hawkins and Lindsey Sodano

Pandia Press
Mount Dora, FL

www.pandiapress.com

History Quest: Early Times Study Guide by Lisa Hawkins and Lindsey Sodano

ISBN 978-1-7334441-0-1

TABLE OF CONTENTS

HOW TO USE THIS STUDY GUIDE

Dear Educator,

Get ready for a fun and enlightening year studying ancient civilizations with *History Quest*! Together, you and your child will travel back in time (and all over the world) to meet all sorts of historical figures. You'll whip up delicious dishes, try your hand at writing in ancient languages, and even make your own mummy. With the *History Quest: Early Times Study Guide*, your child will explore, discover, create, and show off their growing knowledge of the ancient world.

Can I change things up?

Yes! This study guide is full of choices, recommendations, and options to help you customize your studies to fit your child's interests and abilities. For example, many of our craft activities include more than one option for how to get the job done. We've also included three different ways to assess your child's learning—discussion questions, narration, and copywork/dictation. Feel free to use the options that fit best with your child's learning style. However, we highly recommend that you follow the units in the order they are presented.

How should I organize my child's work?

Your child will be doing written work, mapwork, creating various crafts and projects, and completing a History Travel Log, among other things. We recommend setting up a 3-ring history notebook with lined and/or blank paper. With every unit, students start a new section in their history notebooks with the unit's History Travel Log page followed by written work (short answers, narration, copywork, etc.), project photos (photos might be easier than cluttering your household with ziggurats and rotting apple mummies!), and mapwork. A one-inch 3-ring binder should be sufficient.

How does a typical week work?

We've set up a 5-day schedule for each unit, but please feel free to adapt this if you plan to do history on a different schedule. On Day 1 (Discover), you will read from *The Usborne Encyclopedia of World History with Internet Links* and *History Quest: Early Times,* and complete mapwork during some weeks. On Day 2 (Explore), you will read the History Hop time travel component of the *History Quest* chapter, complete the History Travel Log page for the unit, and explore a historical site on Google Earth during some weeks. Day 3 (Create) is most everyone's favorite day—project day! Create day involves a mix of art, architecture, cooking, and other activities to enhance and personalize your child's understanding of the material. On Day 4 (Demonstrate), you have a few different options for how to assess your child's understanding. We have reserved Day 5 (Enrich) for optional enrichment time—exploring websites and reading additional books on the subject.

What is the History Travel Log . . . and how do I use it?

Every chapter of *History Quest* includes a History Hop where your child will imagine traveling back in time to an ancient civilization to meet with real or mythical people from history. The History Travel Log pages will help your child recall and internalize what they learn on each trip. Each week, after reading the History Hop, your child will add a travel log page to their history notebook. You will need a total of 26 History Travel Log pages (Appendix C) during the course for the year. It might be a good idea to print/copy them now so you have them handy. We have also included illustrations for children to color, cut, and paste or tape in their travel log. Alternatively, children could draw and color their own illustrations on their travel logs. Visit www.pandiapress.com/historytravellog for a free PDF of the travel log for printing.

To complete a History Travel Log page:

1. Fill in the blank with the name of the region or civilization visited. You can find this within the text of the History Hop in *History Quest*.
2. Draw an arrow on the map that starts where you live and ends at an X at the place you visited. This helps reinforce geography concepts. Color the map if desired.
3. Draw an arrow on the timeline from the present day to the approximate date of the History Hop. *History Quest* includes a similar timeline illustration that should help pinpoint the correct date. To add a math exercise, calculate how many "years ago" you hopped back in history and write this number under the arrow. Timeline work will help your child visualize how long ago the events occurred. Example:

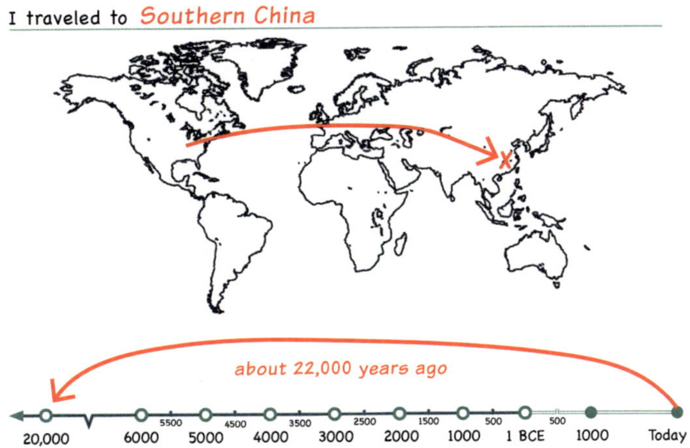

4. At the bottom of the travel log page, there is space to either draw an original illustration or color/cut/paste a provided illustration (Appendix C). Choose based on your child's skill level and interest in drawing.
5. The second page includes a space to fill in the name of the place you visited, who you met, what you saw, and something you learned there. For younger students, you may want to have them dictate their answers while you write the words.

What is Hygge History . . . and how do I pronounce that?

The four Hygge History weeks are loosely based on the Danish concept of hygge [HUE-guh or HOO-guh]. This wonderful word doesn't directly translate to English, but the closest translation would be "a feeling of cozy well-being." Think candles, hot cocoa, and snuggling by a warm fireplace. We want to give you and your child the chance to enjoy these four weeks of ancient literature (which are interspersed throughout the year) without worksheets or assignments of any kind. Just get cozy and enjoy this time reading together before returning to your formal studies the following week.

How can I use this curriculum with a student with a disability?

The best way to adapt the curriculum for a child with a disability is be aware of their specific needs and use instructional scaffolding to support their learning. You may need to set up supports that allow you to meet your child at their current level and help them grow and learn. For example, if using regular scissors is too difficult or dangerous, using loop scissors might be a better option to help your child improve their fine motor skills. Perhaps your child struggles to sit through an entire chapter reading. You could break up the readings into multiple "chunks" throughout the day with gross motor breaks in between.

How can I use this study guide with children in different age groups?

Because this program is so flexible, it's actually quite easy to use simultaneously with students of different ages and abilities, with a target age group of first to fourth grade. For example, you could read the *History Quest* chapter book aloud to younger students, but have older/more-advanced students read it independently. Similarly, you could go over the discussion questions orally with younger students, while asking older students to write out their answers.

Helpful Tips

- You might save time if you print/copy items such as maps and History Travel Log sheets for the entire course all at once and just keep them handy in your history notebook. Visit www.pandiapress.com/historytravellog for a free PDF of the travel log for printing.
- In Appendix B you will find a list of all of the required and additional literature books mentioned in this study guide. Bring this list with you on your next library visit, use it to order books through interlibrary loan, or select titles to purchase books from Amazon.
- Many units—on Day 2, Explore—include suggestions for areas to view on Google Earth that your child encounters while reading *History Quest*. You can use either the Google Earth website (on Chrome) or the tablet (such as iPad) app. It's often fun to start at your own home and "travel" around the world on Google Earth. Start by typing in your address so you can see your home from above, and then type in the new search term to watch yourself "fly" around the planet.
- Ancient history includes topics that could upset some children. The readings for this course were designed with the needs of children in mind, but there are still instances of violence/war, injustices against many groups of people, and some squeamish situations such as mummification. You may want to preview readings before sharing them with your child.
- This course covers the ways in which religion shaped historical events, as well as how some of the world's major religions got started during ancient times. Your child might become curious about the beliefs of various religions, which could lead to some great conversations.
- This book contains 26 units that include a hands-on project. But we all know that life happens. You will have those weeks here and there where there's an emergency dental appointment, the car is in the shop, or there's a power outage in your neighborhood. If you don't get a chance to create a painting of the Ishtar Gate that week, your child is not going to grow up to flunk Western Civ. in college. Think of it this way—most elementary-age kids don't even get a chance to study ancient civilizations at school at all. A missed craft or exercise here and there is not a big deal in the grand scheme of things.
- There is a Notes section found at the end of many units. This is space for you to write planning notes and record your child's learning experience. Some Notes sections include notations by the authors concerning the historicity of the assigned readings and pedagogical strategies.
- Grammar note: This study guide uses singular "they."

We wish you a wonderful year of learning and creating. Now on to the History Quest!

Required Book List

Main Spines

1. ***History Quest: Early Times*** by Lisa Hawkins (ISBN 978-0-9977963-9-1)
2. ***The Usborne Encyclopedia of World History with Internet Links*** (ISBN 978-0794528331)

Hygge History Literature

There are four units in this study guide that employ the Danish concept of hygge—a joyful mix of coziness, togetherness, and a general feeling of well-being—where enjoyment of classic literature is your only assignment for the week. You'll notice that for three of the weeks you have options. Generally speaking, the first option listed is recommended for older elementary students, but we recommend that you read the detailed descriptions of each option found in its corresponding Hygge History unit before choosing.

1. Gilgamesh (Sumer)

Gilgamesh the Hero by Geraldine McCaughrean (ISBN 978-0802852625)

or choose,

The Gilgamesh story told in a series of three books by Ludmila Zeman:

Gilgamesh the King (ISBN 978-0887764370)
The Revenge of Ishtar (ISBN 978-0887764363)
The Last Quest of Gilgamesh (ISBN 978-0887763809)

2. Greek Mythology

Black Ships Before Troy by Rosemary Sutcliff (ISBN 978-0385310697)

or choose,

D'Aulaires' Book of Greek Myths by Ingri d'Aulaire and Edgar Parin d'Aulaire (ISBN 978-0440406945)

3. The *Ramayana* (ancient Indian epic and Hindu mythology)

Ramayana: Divine Loophole by Sanjay Patel (ISBN 978-0811871075)

4. Chinese Mythology

Chinese Children's Favorite Stories by Mingmei Yip (ISBN 978-0804850179)

or choose any number of the following by Li Jian,

The Water Dragon: A Chinese Legend (ISBN 978-1602209787)
The Snake Goddess Colors the World (ISBN 978-1602209824)
The Horse and the Mysterious Drawing (ISBN 978-1602209848)
The Sheep Beauty (ISBN 978-1602209886)
The Little Monkey King's Journey (ISBN 978-1602209817)
The Magical Rooster (ISBN 978-1602209954)
The Bronze Dog (ISBN 978-1602209985)
The Little Pigs and the Sweet Rice Cakes (ISBN 978-1602204539)
The Little Rat and the Golden Seed (ISBN: 978-1602204591)

Master Supply List

Below is an alphabetized list of the supplies needed for all of the craft activities (Day 3: Create) found in the Study Guide. Refer to the individual units for more detailed information about the supplies including quantities needed.

- ☐ 3-ring binder
- ☐ Apples, preferably Granny Smith
- ☐ Asafetida powder (optional)
- ☐ Baker's chocolate
- ☐ Baking soda
- ☐ Bowls
- ☐ Broccoli
- ☐ Broth
- ☐ Butcher paper or long paper
- ☐ Butter
- ☐ Card stock
- ☐ Cardboard
- ☐ Cardboard boxes of various sizes
- ☐ Carrots
- ☐ Chili powder
- ☐ Cilantro, fresh
- ☐ Cinnamon
- ☐ Clay pot
- ☐ Clay, natural/neutral color
- ☐ Clay, silver color or paint silver
- ☐ Coloring pencils
- ☐ Construction paper
- ☐ Cooking oil
- ☐ Cooking utensils
- ☐ Coriander powder
- ☐ Cornstarch
- ☐ Craft glue
- ☐ Craft sticks
- ☐ Cucumber
- ☐ Cumin powder
- ☐ Cumin seeds
- ☐ Decorative tape
- ☐ Egg carton
- ☐ Eggshells
- ☐ Flat rock/pan/pizza stone
- ☐ Garam masala
- ☐ Garlic, fresh
- ☐ Ginger, fresh
- ☐ Green chilies, fresh or canned
- ☐ Ground meat, or vegetarian equivalent
- ☐ Hammer or can for crushing
- ☐ Heat source
- ☐ Hole punch
- ☐ Honey or other sweetener
- ☐ Index cards, blank and preferably colored
- ☐ Items to decorate a ziggurat scene (optional), e.g. animal, plant, and people figurines
- ☐ Markers
- ☐ Mask decorations (optional)
- ☐ Metallic paints
- ☐ Milk
- ☐ Mortar and pestle (optional)
- ☐ Naan bread (optional)
- ☐ One-gallon storage bags
- ☐ Onions
- ☐ Paintbrushes
- ☐ Painting surface, paper or stone
- ☐ Paints
- ☐ Pan (large) or wok
- ☐ Paper
- ☐ Paper fastener/brad
- ☐ Paper plates
- ☐ Paper towel tubes
- ☐ Pencil
- ☐ Pictures of animals
- ☐ Plastic spoon
- ☐ Poster board
- ☐ Protein of your choice
- ☐ Quart-size storage bags
- ☐ Red bell pepper
- ☐ Red kidney beans
- ☐ Rice
- ☐ Rubber bands
- ☐ Ruler
- ☐ Salt, for flavoring
- ☐ Sand (optional)
- ☐ Scissors
- ☐ Small play pieces, e.g. pebbles, pennies, buttons
- ☐ Small, light objects to launch, e.g. mini marshmallows
- ☐ Soy sauce
- ☐ Stick with a pointed end
- ☐ String
- ☐ Table salt, large container for apple mummification
- ☐ Tape
- ☐ Tissue paper or newspaper
- ☐ Tomatoes
- ☐ Tools for grinding
- ☐ Turmeric
- ☐ Vanilla extract
- ☐ Vinegar, rice or white
- ☐ Water
- ☐ Wedge shape tool, small
- ☐ Whole wheat berries or stone-ground wheat flour
- ☐ Wine cork or empty thread spool
- ☐ Wooden dowels or chopsticks
- ☐ Yogurt, plain

INTRODUCTION

WHAT IS HISTORY?

This Week's Quest

Learn the definition of ancient history.

Resources & Materials

History Quest: Early Times (HQ)

Usborne Encyclopedia of World History with Internet Links (UEWH)

My Early Times History Notebook cover page (Appendix C)

Enrichment Reading

Archaeologists Dig For Clues by Kate Duke

Fossils Tell of Long Ago by Aliki

Supplies Needed for Day 3

- History 3-ring binder
- Hole punch
- Coloring tools

Unit Schedule

Day 1 Discover	Day 2 Explore	Day 3 Create	Day 4 Demonstrate	Day 5 Enrich
UEWH pages 12–91	HQ Introduction	Create your History Notebook	Review Terms & Concepts	Explore Pandia Web Links
	Google Earth		Complete one or more review options	Read from Enrichment Reading list
	Plan a prehistory field trip			

Terms & Concepts

The Big Ideas

- History–the study of the past
- Ancient–very old

The Details

- Scientists estimate that the universe is about 15 billion years old, and Earth is about 4.6 billion years old.
- Primates–a group of mammals that includes lemurs, monkeys, apes, and humans
- Some primates began walking upright about five million years ago. Over a very, very long amount of time, they eventually evolved into modern humans.

Lessons

Day 1. Discover

- ☐ **Read pages 12–91 in UEWH.** If desired, navigate to some of the websites recommended in the book. Spend as much time as your child wants exploring these pages on prehistory. It is certainly not necessary to read everything. This section of the book gives a wonderful overview of what was happening on our planet from the Big Bang up until the Paleolithic era. Some of the creatures are quite striking. Early elementary children are often fascinated by the Meganeura, a dragonfly-like creature with a two-foot wingspan, the Platybelodon with its giant teeth, and, of course, the dinosaurs. Again, there is no need to read every word in this lengthy section. You can still move on to the next unit without having finished this section.

Day 2. Explore

- ☐ **Read the Introduction in HQ pages 1–3.** *Note: The page numbers given in this study guide for* History Quest *refer to the printed and PDF versions of the book. EPUB and Kindle (MOBI) versions have varying page numbers. For those publications, readings can be located using the chapter and History Hop titles.*
- ☐ **Google Earth.** Search for "Lascaux" and click on the image to see some of the cave paintings.
- ☐ **Plan a prehistory themed field trip.** This is completely optional, of course, but if you happen to live within reasonable traveling distance of a museum of natural history, why not schedule a field trip? A few museums in the United States with excellent collections include the following:

  The Field Museum of Natural History, Chicago, IL
  Fernbank Museum of Natural History, Atlanta, GA
  Wyoming Dinosaur Center, Thermopolis, WY
  Smithsonian Institution, National Museum of Natural History, Washington, D.C.

Day 3. Create

- ☐ **Create Your History Notebook**

Supplies:

- My Early Times History Notebook cover page (Appendix C)
- History 3-ring binder
- Hole punch
- Coloring tools

Directions:

Write your name on and color the cover page; make it the cover or the first page of your history notebook.

Every chapter of *History Quest* includes a History Hop where your child will travel back in time to an ancient civilization and meet with a real or imaginary person from that time. Each week, after reading the History Hop, your child will complete the corresponding History Travel Log page. The travel log pages include a coloring activity based on the History Hop. If your child is interested in art, they could choose to draw their own illustration instead.

Future Supply Alert: Coming up in Unit 2, you may want to purchase wheat berries for the bread-making craft. These are available at some natural food stores, and also online. If you buy them online, you may want to purchase them fairly soon so they will arrive on time to bake Neolithic bread.

Day 4. Demonstrate

☐ **Read through the Terms & Concepts.** Optional: Copy some or all of the Terms & Concepts into your history notebook.

☐ **Complete one or more of the following** in order to strengthen your child's knowledge of the material and to provide an opportunity for you to evaluate their understanding:

Option #1 Short Answers

Answer the following questions verbally or write them in your history notebook:

Q: What is history?
A: History is the study of the past.

Q: What does the word *ancient* mean?
A: Ancient means very old.

Q: Did people and dinosaurs live at the same time?
A: No. The dinosaurs went extinct long before people evolved.

Option #2 Narration

Answer the following verbally or in writing:

- List three important things you learned about history and prehistoric times.

Option #3 Copywork/Dictation

Copy or write from dictation one of the following into your history notebook:

History is the study of the past.

Humans evolved hundreds of thousands of years ago. People who study human history are called historians.

Day 5. Enrich

- ☐ **Visit www.pandiapress.com/weblinks.** There you will find a description of some recommended websites related to this unit.
- ☐ **Read one or more from the Enrichment Reading list**

  Archaeologists Dig For Clues by Kate Duke. Written in the style of *Magic School Bus*, this comic-style book follows a group of schoolchildren learning about the work archaeologists do. Contains some good technical information about archaeology.

  Fossils Tell of Long Ago by Aliki. This book is a great connection between science and history, with Aliki's friendly illustrations showing how various types of fossils are created.

Unit Notes

UNIT 1

PALEOLITHIC TIMES

This Week's Quest

Learn about Paleolithic times when groups of nomads traveled constantly in search of food—while trying not to *become* food—in the challenging climate at the end of the last Ice Age.

Resources & Materials

History Quest: Early Times (HQ)

Usborne Encyclopedia of World History with Internet Links (UEWH)

Map 1 (Appendix C)

History Travel Log page and The Knapper illustration (Appendix C)

Enrichment Reading

Discovery in the Cave by Mark Dubowski

The Secret Cave: Discovering Lascaux by Emily Arnold McCully

The First Drawing by Mordicai Gerstein

Supplies Needed for Day 3

Option 1

- Clay pot
- One-gallon storage bags
- Hammer or can for crushing
- Vegetable oil
- Paintbrushes
- Painting surface (paper or stone)
- Mortar and pestle (optional)

Option 2

- Paints
- Painting surface (paper or stone)
- Paintbrushes

Unit Schedule

Day 1 **Discover**	Day 2 **Explore**	Day 3 **Create**	Day 4 **Demonstrate**	Day 5 **Enrich**
UEWH pages 92–99	History Hop! The Knapper	Create a Paleolithic Cave Painting	Review Terms & Concepts	Explore Pandia Web Links
HQ Chapter 1 Paleolithic Times	History Travel Log		Complete one or more review options	Read from Enrichment Reading list
Map 1				

Terms & Concepts

The Big Ideas

- Prehistoric–the period in the past before people learned how to write
- Artifacts–things made by people in the past that help reveal what life was like in the past
- Archaeologists–people who study history and prehistory by looking for artifacts at sites around the world
- Paleolithic era–people invented tools made of stones, including axes and stone-tipped spears. They lived by hunting wild animals and gathering wild food.

The Details

- Nomadic–a lifestyle where people move around from place to place instead of settling in one place
- Hunter-gatherers–people who survived by moving from place to place to hunt wild animals and forage for wild food
- The Paleolithic era, also known as the Stone Age, ended about 12,000 years ago.
- Some Paleolithic people discovered how to domesticate (or tame) wolves to help them with their hunting and how to use fire to help them survive.

Lessons

Day 1. Discover

- ☐ **Read pages 92–99 in UEWH.** If desired, navigate to some of the websites recommended in the book.
- ☐ **Read Chapter 1: Paleolithic Times in HQ pages 5–10**
- ☐ **Complete Map 1.** Referring to a world map or globe, label the following. (Map keys are located in Appendix A.) This is a great time to introduce proper map labeling to your child. When labeling a map, the names of continents and countries should be in all caps (e.g. AFRICA, JAPAN). Cities should be indicated with a dot (•). Optionally, when labeling modern-day places on maps of the ancient world, put the name of the modern-day location in brackets to show that the area did not have this name during ancient times (e.g. [SPAIN], [PAKISTAN]).

1. Label these continents:

   NORTH AMERICA
   SOUTH AMERICA
   AFRICA
   ANTARCTICA
   AUSTRALIA
   EUROPE
   ASIA

2. Label these bodies of water:

   Atlantic Ocean
   Pacific Ocean
   Arctic Ocean
   Southern Ocean
   Indian Ocean

3. Draw a star where you live.

4. Draw a compass rose in an open area of the map (arrows with N, S, E, and W to show direction).

Day 2. Explore

- ☐ **Read History Hop! The Knapper in HQ pages 11–17**
- ☐ **History Travel Log.** Complete the travel log page for this unit and place it in your history notebook. Refer to "How to Use this Study Guide" (page 6) for instructions on how to complete a History Travel Log page.

Day 3. Create

- ☐ **Craft: Create a Paleolithic Cave Painting.** There are two versions of this craft, choose depending on how much time you have and how much mess you can tolerate.

Supplies:

Option 1 (For those who don't mind a bit of a mess)

- Small red clay pot
- 2 one-gallon storage bags
- Hammer or can for crushing
- Vegetable oil
- Paintbrushes
- Painting surface (paper or stone)
- Optional: mortar and pestle

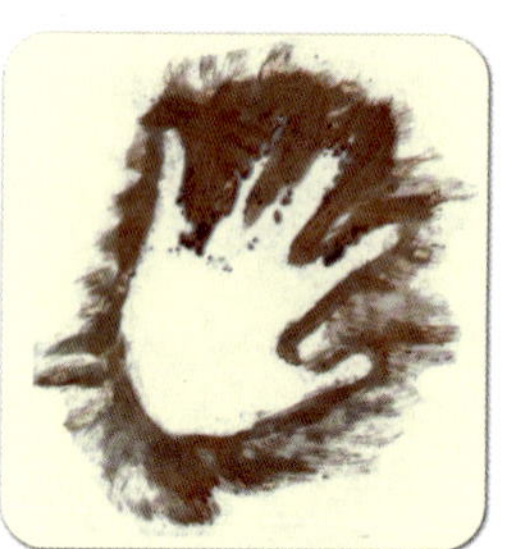

Option 2 (A quicker version with less mess)

- Paints
- Painting surface/paper
- Paintbrushes

Directions:

Be sure to discuss the topic of cave painting with your child, asking them how they think Paleolithic people invented the paints in the first place, how they might have created different colors, and even why they would want to spend time doing this sort of activity. You can find examples of these cave paintings in the *Usborne Encyclopedia*, or image search "Lascaux" on the internet.

Make your own cave paint (if you choose Option 1): We strongly suggest doing this outdoors. Supervise your child as they place the red clay pot in a gallon storage bag (we recommend placing that bag into a second bag since the bag might tear during the grinding process). Break the pot into pieces as small as you can get them using a hammer and/or heavy can. Help your child carefully pour these pieces into the mortar and use the pestle to grind the pieces into a fine powder. If you don't own a mortar and pestle, a heavy can and a plate or bowl should work well. Add some vegetable oil (start with about one tablespoon and see if you need to add more) and mix in until you end up with a gritty sort of paint consistency.

If you are choosing Option 2, set out your premade paints for your child to use.

Now it is time to paint! Encourage your child to paint the sort of pictures Paleolithic people would have painted. You can use a paintbrush, or to be more authentic—thin sticks, feathers, or even fingers. You can have your child paint on paper taped to a wall (outdoors!), or perhaps wide, flat stones for a more accurate idea of how challenging cave painting would have been.

Day 4. Demonstrate

- ☐ **Read through the Terms & Concepts.** Optional: Copy some or all of the Terms & Concepts into your history notebook.
- ☐ **Complete one or more of the following** in order to strengthen your child's knowledge of the material and to provide an opportunity for you to evaluate their understanding:

Option #1 Short Answers

Answer the following questions verbally or write them in your history notebook:

Q: What was the weather like for the Paleolithic people, and how did they make themselves comfortable in that weather?

A: *The weather was cold. They wore clothing made of animal skins.*

Q: What tools did the Paleolithic people learn how to use? If you could give them one tool to help make their lives easier, what would that be? (Be sure to explain that a tool is anything people use to make work easier.)

A: *Paleolithic people used knapped tools made from stones.* (Answers will vary for the second part of the question.)

Q: What animal did the Paleolithic people make friends with and learn to domesticate?

A: *The people made friends with wolves. Those wolves are the ancestors of dogs.*

Q: What do you think life would have been like for Paleolithic people if they never discovered how to control fire?

A: *Answers will vary: They would have to eat raw meat, they would not have light at night, etc.*

Option #2 Narration

Answer the following verbally or in writing:

- List three important things you learned about the Paleolithic era.

Option #3 Copywork/Dictation

Copy or write from dictation one of the following into your history notebook:

In Paleolithic times, people ate wild plants and worked with wolves to hunt animals.

The Paleolithic era was many thousands of years ago. People had to hunt animals and eat wild plants. Paleolithic means "old stone age." People at this time did not know how to write or how to farm. They did not build houses, but they learned how to domesticate wolves.

Day 5. Enrich

- ☐ **Visit www.pandiapress.com/weblinks.** There you will find a description of some recommended websites related to this unit.
- ☐ **Read one or more from the Enrichment Reading list**

  Discovery in the Cave by Mark Dubowski (a Step Into Reading book, Level 4). This is a wonderfully illustrated true story of the children who first discovered the now-famous cave paintings in Lascaux, France, during World War II. Highly recommended.

  The Secret Cave: Discovering Lascaux by Emily Arnold McCully. Another rendition of the story of the group of young boys who first discovered the cave paintings at Lascaux.

  The First Drawing by Mordicai Gerstein. This book transports readers back to Paleolithic times to learn the fictional story of a Paleolithic boy with a talent for art.

UNIT 2

NEOLITHIC TIMES

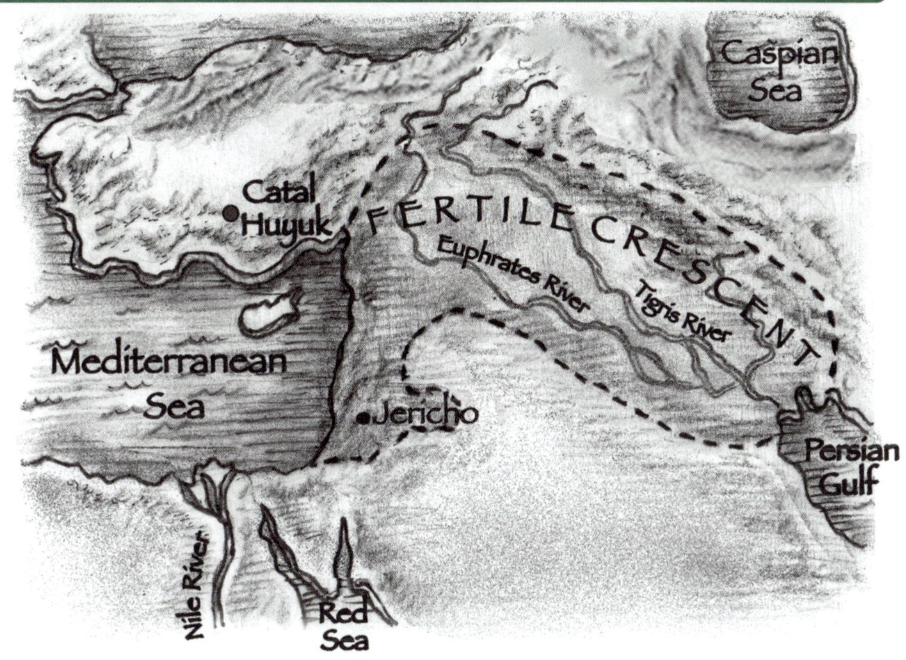

This Week's Quest

Learn about Neolithic times, a time when people stopped chasing their food and started growing it instead.

Resources & Materials

History Quest: Early Times (HQ)

Usborne Encyclopedia of World History with Internet Links (UEWH)

Map 2 (Appendix C)

History Travel Log page and The Stone Toolmakers illustration (Appendix C)

Enrichment Reading

Stone Age Boy by Satoshi Kitamura

Skara Brae: The Story of a Prehistoric Village by Olivier Dunrea

Supplies Needed for Day 3

Option 1

- Whole wheat berries (1 to 2 cups)
- Water
- Tools for grinding
- Heat source
- Flat rock/pan/pizza stone
- Other optional ingredients

Option 2

- Stone-ground wheat flour (1 to 2 cups)
- Water
- Heat source
- Flat rock/pan/pizza stone
- Other optional ingredients

Unit Schedule

Day 1 Discover	Day 2 Explore	Day 3 Create	Day 4 Demonstrate	Day 5 Enrich
UEWH pages 100–109	History Hop! The Stone Toolmakers	Bake Neolithic Bread	Review Terms & Concepts	Explore Pandia Web Links
HQ Chapter 2 Neolithic Times	Google Earth		Complete one or more review options	Read from Enrichment Reading list
Map 2	History Travel Log			

Terms & Concepts

The Big Ideas

- Neolithic people domesticated animals to live on farms so they could use the animals for many resources: milk and meat for food, wool and skins for clothing, and horns and bone for tools.

- During the Neolithic era, people made new kinds of tools that worked better and lasted longer.

- The Fertile Crescent is the region in the Middle East where people first discovered farming. Fertile means that things grow well in that region. A crescent is a shape like a curved *C*.

The Details

- The Neolithic era happened at different times in different places around the world and lasted for thousands of years.

- One of the big changes in the Neolithic era was that people began to farm their own food instead of mostly hunting animals and gathering plants.

- The oldest known city in the world is Catal Huyuk, located in present-day Turkey.

Lessons

Day 1. Discover

☐ **Read pages 100–109 in UEWH.** If desired, navigate to some of the websites recommended in the book.

☐ **Read Chapter 2: Neolithic Times in HQ pages 19–27**

☐ **Begin Map 2.*** Referring to the map in HQ on page 19 label the following.

Note: The page numbers given in this study guide for maps found in History Quest *refer to the printed and PDF versions of the book. EPUB and Kindle (MOBI) versions have varying page numbers. For those publications, maps can be located using the Table of Maps index found at the end of* History Quest.

1. Label these bodies of water:

    Mediterranean Sea
    Red Sea
    Caspian Sea
    Nile River
    Tigris River
    Euphrates River

2. Label these cities:

    •Catal Huyuk
    •Jericho

3. Shade the Fertile Crescent.

* Map 2 is started in this unit. Additional entries are added to Map 2 in Unit 6 (Egypt: Part Two).

Day 2. Explore

☐ **Read History Hop! The Stone Toolmakers in HQ pages 28–32**

☐ **Google Earth.** Search for "Catalhoyuk" and click on the image of the dig site to see more pictures.

☐ **History Travel Log.** Complete the travel log page for this unit and place it in your history notebook.

Day 3. Create

☐ **Cooking: Bake Neolithic Bread.** There are two versions of this craft. Choose depending on whether you are able to obtain whole wheat berries. You might be able to find them at a natural foods store, but if not, feel free to use premade stone-ground wheat flour.

Supplies:

Option 1 (Using whole wheat berries)

- 1 to 2 cups whole wheat berries
- Water
- Tools for grinding: mortar and pestle; heavy, flat rocks; sturdy cutting board; and/or a heavy can
- Heat source: grill, firepit, or oven
- Flat rock/pan/pizza stone for baking
- Optional: historically appropriate ingredients like butter, milk, herbs, nuts, salt

Option 2 (Using stone-ground wheat flour)

- 1 to 2 cups stone-ground wheat flour
- Water
- Heat source: grill, firepit, or oven
- Flat rock/pan/pizza stone for baking
- Optional: historically appropriate ingredients like butter, milk, herbs, nuts, salt

Directions:

Prepare to make your own Neolithic bread. If you choose Option 1, buy some whole wheat berries at your local natural foods store (or online). Spending the time grinding wheat berries by hand will show your child how labor-intensive this process truly was. It's fine if you just grind a little of the flour and add it to already-prepared flour (buy stone-ground wheat flour if you're not going to grind all of the berries yourself). Have your child use a mortar and pestle, flat rocks, or a heavy can and a sturdy base like a wooden cutting board. This is difficult work and it can be messy. The idea is to give this a try and learn firsthand how tough this task was for Neolithic people. You want to end up with about 2 cups of flour.

Once you have flour, either produced (Option 1) or purchased (Option 2), pour it into a bowl and mix with enough water to produce a sticky but workable dough. It should take about 1¼ cups of water. You can ask your child if there are any ingredients that the Neolithic people could have added to the dough at this point to make it tastier. Butter, milk, herbs, and nuts would be appropriate. During the Neolithic era, people started using and trading salt, so salt would technically be an appropriate addition. Divide up your dough into three or four pieces and mix ingredients into however many pieces you want. For example, you could make a completely plain one, another salted, and the remainder mixed with other ingredients, like a little butter and/or herbs. Flatten the dough into disks about ½ inch to 1 inch thick. You could use a knife to mark the bread so you remember which ingredients are in each piece (e.g. "S" for salt).

It's time to bake! Preheat your oven to 450 degrees. Place a baking stone (such as a pizza stone) or a seasoned/oiled cast-iron pan in the oven and allow that to heat up. Bake your dough until browned, about 10–15 minutes. Let cool and enjoy. For an extra authentic experience, instead of using your oven, fire up a grill. If you want to get even closer to authenticity light a campfire and prop a platter-like flat stone near the edge of the fire and let that heat up and cook the dough there.

Day 4. Demonstrate

☐ **Read through the Terms & Concepts.** Optional: Copy some or all of the Terms & Concepts into your history notebook.

☐ **Complete one or more of the following** in order to strengthen your child's knowledge of the material and to provide an opportunity for you to evaluate their understanding:

Option #1 Short Answers

Answer the following questions verbally or write them in your history notebook:

Q: Why did Neolithic people want to live near rivers?

A: *The land near rivers is more fertile, so the people could grow crops there.*

Q: What are some of the resources that people were able to get from the animals they tamed on their farms?

A: *The people could get meat and milk for food, and wool and skins to make their clothing. They also made tools out of horns and bones.*

Q: Neolithic people began to learn how to make pottery out of the clay-like mud they could get near rivers. How could pottery help the Neolithic people make their lives easier?

A: *With pottery, the people could store or carry water and food.*

Q: If your family was Paleolithic—wandering around in search of food—and you discovered there was a large group of Neolithic people nearby, would you tell your family that they should join the Neolithic people, or stay Paleolithic? Why?

A: *Answers will vary.*

Option #2 Narration

Answer the following verbally or in writing:

- List three important things you learned about the Neolithic era.

Option #3 Copywork/Dictation

Copy or write from dictation one of the following into your history notebook:

In the Neolithic era, people grew their own food and tamed animals to live on their farms.

The Neolithic era came after the Paleolithic era. People learned how to tame animals for their farms. They learned how to grow their own food and make better tools out of stone. Neolithic means "new stone age." People at this time did not write, but they did build houses.

Day 5. Enrich

- ☐ **Visit www.pandiapress.com/weblinks.** There you will find a description of some recommended websites related to this unit.
- ☐ **Read one or more from the Enrichment Reading list.**

  Stone Age Boy by Satoshi Kitamura. A pleasant imaginary story about a modern-day boy who travels back in time and hangs out with a Neolithic family. There's not a lot of historical information, and the Neolithic family seems much better groomed and dressed than one would think, but children might enjoy this fictional portrayal of life in the New Stone Age.

  Skara Brae: The Story of a Prehistoric Village by Olivier Dunrea. This book tells about the Neolithic village of Skara Brae, located in the islands just north of Scotland. Black-and-white illustrations focus on the architecture of the homes and village.

UNIT 3

CIVILIZATIONS BEGIN

This Week's Quest

Learn what actually makes a civilization. What did people need to do in order to live together in an organized way?

Resources & Materials

History Quest: Early Times (HQ)

Usborne Encyclopedia of World History with Internet Links (UEWH)

History Travel Log page and The Scribes illustration (Appendix C)

Cuneiform Alphabet (Appendix C)

Supplies Needed for Day 3

- Clay, natural/neutral color
- Stick-shaped item with a pointed end
- Item that can make a small wedge shape

Enrichment Reading

Life in Ancient Mesopotamia by Shilpa Mehta-Jones

DK Eyewitness Books: Ancient Civilizations by Joseph Fullman

You Wouldn't Want to Live Without Writing! by Roger Canavan

Unit Schedule

Day 1 Discover	Day 2 Explore	Day 3 Create	Day 4 Demonstrate	Day 5 Enrich
UEWH pages 110–112	History Hop! The Scribes	Make Your Own Cuneiform Tablet	Review Terms & Concepts	Explore Pandia Web Links
HQ Chapter 3 Civilizations Begin	History Travel Log		Complete one or more review options	Read from Enrichment Reading list

Terms & Concepts

The Big Ideas

❋ A civilization is a place where a very large group of people live and work together.

❋ Civilizations have specialization, which is when people do many different kinds of jobs instead of everyone being a farmer.

❋ Each civilization has a government that comes up with rules and makes sure people follow those rules.

The Details

❋ Civilizations have hierarchy, which means that not everyone has the same amount of power. Usually a few people have most of the power and most of the people have very little power.

❋ All ancient civilizations were religious, which means they had beliefs about gods or forces that made things happen in the world. Most civilizations were polytheistic, which means that they believed in many gods.

❋ Every civilization figured out a way to write things down so they could keep track of things that were important to them.

Lessons

Day 1. Discover

- ☐ **Read pages 110–112 in UEWH.** If desired, navigate to some of the websites recommended in the book.
- ☐ **Read Chapter 3: Civilizations Begin in HQ pages 33–40**

Day 2. Explore

- ☐ **Read History Hop! The Scribes in HQ pages 41–46**
- ☐ **History Travel Log.** Complete the travel log page for this unit and place it in your history notebook.

Day 3. Create

- ☐ **Craft: Make Your Own Cuneiform Tablet**

Supplies:

- Clay, preferably in a natural/neutral color: Sculpey, air-dry clay, or clay alternative (e.g. Crayola Model Magic)
- A stick-shaped item with a pointed end, like a chopstick or a pencil
- An item that can make a small wedge shape: a pie-shaped game piece from the board game Trivial Pursuit, a drinking straw bent into a wedge shape (a thicker smoothie straw will hold the shape a bit better than a regular straw), or even the triangle-shaped edge of a set of nail clippers (with supervision)
- Cuneiform Alphabet (Appendix C)

Directions:
Take a piece of modeling clay and form the cuneiform tablet. It should be about half an inch thick. Many cuneiform tablets fit the size of the scribe's hand (about the size of a smartphone), but we recommend making yours bigger so it is easier for your child to work with. The choice of size depends on what your child decides to write.

Before your child starts creating their cuneiform word or message, you may want to lightly score lines into the clay as a guide to help them leave a little space between each separate cuneiform character.

Use the Cuneiform Alphabet key to plan out your message. Your child can work on their initials or name, a message to a parent, or even a secret message that someone else has to decode.

Using the stick and wedge shapes, press the design into the clay. Originally, cuneiform was written in just about every direction possible, but for simplicity's sake, we would recommend you move left to right or top to bottom.

If using clay that needs to be baked, follow the directions on the box to bake the clay.

Alternative: If you don't have clay available, your child can follow the cuneiform alphabet and simply write out a cuneiform message onto a piece of paper. Or, you can write your child a message and have them decode it for you.

Day 4. Demonstrate

- ☐ **Read through the Terms & Concepts.** Optional: Copy some or all of the Terms & Concepts into your history notebook.
- ☐ **Complete one or more of the following** in order to strengthen your child's knowledge of the material and to provide an opportunity for you to evaluate their understanding:

Option #1 Short Answers

Answer the following questions verbally or write them in your history notebook:

Q: Name at least two different things that are part of every civilization.

A: Answers may include: *Cities, specialized jobs, government, and writing.*

Q: What does *hierarchy* mean?

A: A hierarchy is when a small number of people have lots of power, while most people have very little power.

Q: Why did civilizations have to have governments?

A: Civilizations needed a way to make up rules and make sure the people followed the rules.

Option #2 Narration

Answer the following verbally or in writing:

- List three important things you learned about the beginnings of civilization.

Option #3 Copywork/Dictation

Copy or write from dictation one of the following into your history notebook:

In civilizations, lots of people live together in an organized way.

Civilizations began in the ancient world when a lot of people lived together in the same place. They had cities where people could do many kinds of jobs and buy and sell different things. Every ancient civilization had religious beliefs.

Day 5. Enrich

- ☐ **Visit www.pandiapress.com/weblinks.** There you will find a description of some recommended websites related to this unit.
- ☐ **Read one or more from the Enrichment Reading list**

  Life in Ancient Mesopotamia by Shilpa Mehta-Jones. This book provides a nice overview of various aspects of early Mesopotamian civilizations, covering topics such as geography, daily life, religion, and technology. Excellent pictures.

  DK Eyewitness Books: Ancient Civilizations by Joseph Fullman. This is a typical *DK Eyewitness* book, full of information and wonderful photographs. The content ranges all over the globe in its general coverage of various civilizations.

  You Wouldn't Want to Live Without Writing! by Roger Canavan. Don't be fooled by the silly titles and cartoonish illustrations. The *You Wouldn't Want to…* series of books contains worthwhile historical information and is worth checking out.

Unit Notes

UNIT 4

SUMER

This Week's Quest

Learn about the oldest civilization, Sumer, also known as the civilization that invented something we use every day—the wheel.

Resources & Materials

History Quest: Early Times (HQ)

Usborne Encyclopedia of World History with Internet Links (UEWH)

History Travel Log page and The First Author illustration (Appendix C)

Enrichment Reading

You Wouldn't Want to Be a Sumerian Slave! by Jacqueline Morley

The Sumerians by Jane Shuter

Supplies Needed for Day 3

- Several empty cardboard boxes of various sizes
- Brown paint/painting supplies or brown paper (if the boxes are not brown to begin with)
- Sand (optional)
- Craft glue
- Scissors
- Black marker
- Tape
- Items to decorate your ziggurat scene (optional)

Unit Schedule

Day 1 **Discover**	Day 2 **Explore**	Day 3 **Create**	Day 4 **Demonstrate**	Day 5 **Enrich**
UEWH pages 110–113	History Hop! The First Author	Make a Model Ziggurat	Review Terms & Concepts	Explore Pandia Web Links
HQ Chapter 4 Sumer	Google Earth		Complete one or more review options	Read from Enrichment Reading list
	History Travel Log			

Terms & Concepts

The Big Ideas

❋ The first civilization in the world was the Sumerian civilization in southern Mesopotamia. It began around 6,000 years ago (4000 BCE).

❋ The Sumerians developed the first writing, called cuneiform. *Cuneiform* means "wedge-shaped," because many of the shapes of cuneiform were triangular, like wedges.

The Details

❋ The Sumerians wrote the first epic, called the *Epic of Gilgamesh*. Epics are stories that explore important, big ideas, like the meaning of life and fear of death.

❋ Sumer was conquered by Sargon the Great, who was from the city of Akkad. He started the Akkadian Empire.

❋ The Akkadian Empire existed during the Bronze Age, which was when people learned how to make bronze metal and shape it into tools, replacing many stone tools.

❋ The Sumerians were the first people to figure out how to use the wheel to help them do their work. One of the most important uses of the wheel was in the chariot, a horse-drawn cart that could carry soldiers into battle.

❋ The temples of Sumer were special places dedicated to Sumerian gods. They were called ziggurats.

❋ Enheduanna, the daughter of Sargon, was the high priestess of Ur and the first person in history to sign her name to written literature.

Lessons

Day 1. Discover

- ☐ **Read pages 110–113 in UEWH.** (Pages 110–112 are review.) If desired, navigate to some of the websites recommended in the book.
- ☐ **Read Chapter 4: Sumer in HQ pages 47–55**

Day 2. Explore

- ☐ **Read History Hop! The First Author in HQ pages 56–61**
- ☐ **Google Earth.** Search for "Ziggurat of Ur" and click on the ziggurat image to learn more.
- ☐ **History Travel Log.** Complete the travel log page for this unit and place it in your history notebook.

Day 3. Create

☐ **Craft: Make a Model Ziggurat**

Supplies:

- Several empty cardboard boxes (brown ones will be easiest to paint, but you could also reuse cereal boxes, frozen pizza boxes, cracker boxes, etc. Try to collect several so your child has a few options to choose from in building.)
- Brown butcher or packing paper to wrap your boxes (if the boxes aren't brown), or brown paint and painting supplies if you want to paint the boxes
- Optional: If painting, you could add some sand to your paint to give the surface a more realistic texture
- Craft glue (regular white glue may also work if you don't have craft glue)
- Scissors
- Black marker
- Tape
- Optional: toy people, animals, palm trees, etc. to decorate the scene

Directions:

Offer your child a wide assortment of sizes of boxes to work with. Study the illustration of the ziggurat in the *Usborne Encyclopedia*, or look up pictures of ziggurats online. Take a few minutes to try out different box sizes to build a ziggurat shape. Every level of the ziggurat should be a bit smaller than the one directly under it.

Once you have chosen your boxes, either "gift wrap" them in butcher paper or paint them brown (if they were not brown to begin with). Once ready, use your craft glue to glue the boxes into the ziggurat shape. While this is drying, you could take an unused cardboard box or a piece of a paper shopping bag and cut a long, thin rectangle shape. Bend the rectangle back and forth to create a staircase. Use a black marker to draw doors or other features you would like to include.

Day 4. Demonstrate

- ☐ **Read through the Terms & Concepts.** Optional: Copy some or all of the Terms & Concepts into your history notebook.
- ☐ **Complete one or more of the following** in order to strengthen your child's knowledge of the material and to provide an opportunity for you to evaluate their understanding:

Option #1 Short Answers

Answer the following questions verbally or write them in your history notebook:

Q: What is the name of the kind of writing the Sumerians invented?

A: They invented cuneiform.

Q: Sumerians invented the wheel, which they used for many different activities. How do you think life would be different for us today if no one ever discovered how to use a wheel?

A: Answers may vary. Students might mention that we would need to walk everywhere (no cars, bikes, or carriages).

Option #2 Narration

Answer the following verbally or in writing:

- List three important things you learned about the Sumerian civilization.

Option #3 Copywork/Dictation

Copy or write from dictation one of the following into your history notebook:

The Sumerians invented the wheel, and they also invented writing.

The first place people made a civilization was in Sumer, which is part of Mesopotamia. The Sumerian civilization invented writing. They also invented the wheel. They used bronze to make tools and weapons.

Day 5. Enrich

- ☐ **Visit www.pandiapress.com/weblinks.** There you will find a description of some recommended websites related to this unit.
- ☐ **Read one or more from the Enrichment Reading list**

  You Wouldn't Want to Be a Sumerian Slave! by Jacqueline Morley. This title from the *You Wouldn't Want to Be…* series contains a lot of solid historical content while skillfully drawing the reader into the narrative.

  The Sumerians by Jane Shuter. General overview of Sumerian life and culture.

Unit Notes

HYGGE HISTORY #1

GILGAMESH

Ancient Sumerian carving of Gilgamesh

This Week's Quest

Read and enjoy the story of Gilgamesh.

Resources

Gilgamesh the Hero by Geraldine McCaughrean (ISBN 978-0802852625)

or choose,

The Gilgamesh story told in a series of three books by Ludmila Zeman:

Gilgamesh the King (ISBN 978-0887764370)

The Revenge of Ishtar (978-0887764363)

The Last Quest of Gilgamesh (ISBN 978-0887763809)

Hygge History

Welcome to your first week of Hygge History, where cozy enjoyment of classic literature is your only assignment. The four literature units this year employ the Danish concept of hygge [HUE-guh or HOO-guh], which doesn't translate directly to English—it's a joyful mix of coziness, togetherness, and a general feeling of well-being. So put your pencils down and your feet up. Snuggle up together in a comfy chair with some hot cocoa, or if you happen to be reading this in the fall, grab your pumpkin spice beverage of choice. There are no worksheets or assignments to complete. Just read and enjoy. You're welcome.

Up first is a children's version of the *Epic of Gilgamesh*, considered by many to be the oldest surviving work of literature. This story boasts so many of the ingredients we expect from an epic tale—a hero's journey, a quest for immortality, and the transformative power of love and friendship.

But to avoid an epic fail with your first epic, you are going to want to choose a children's version of the story that is a good fit for your child. We suggest previewing books to make sure you find the appropriate one for your child's level of interest, sensitivity, and maturity. Here are our two picks:

Option 1: *Gilgamesh the Hero* by Geraldine McCaughrean, illustrated by David Parkins

This version is quite a bit longer than the three Zeman books (option 2), so it includes much more detail from the original epic, as well as some lovely poetic language. While the book has some beautiful illustrations interspersed throughout, it is the words, not the pictures, that really tell the story here. Please note that the treatment of the character of Shamhat (called "Hatti" in this version) is more similar to the original text of the epic, which means there is a sex scene that some parents might find inappropriate for their young readers. More advanced/mature readers or those who prefer a poetic style of language might prefer this version over the Zeman series.

Option 2: *Gilgamesh the King, The Revenge of Ishtar*, and *The Last Quest of Gilgamesh*, all retold and illustrated by Ludmila Zeman

These three books are full of absolutely gorgeous illustrations. Zeman tells the story in a way that is friendly to the sensibilities of modern kids. Her treatment of the female character of Shamhat is especially gentle compared to the original text. Younger kids and people who adore fantastic illustrations might prefer this version.

Hygge History Notes

UNIT 5

EGYPT: PART ONE

This Week's Quest

Begin to learn about Ancient Egypt, the land of pyramids, mummies, and pharaohs.

Resources & Materials

History Quest: Early Times (HQ)

Usborne Encyclopedia of World History with Internet Links (UEWH)

History Travel Log page and The Chief Embalmer illustration (Appendix C)

Supplies Needed for Day 3

- Apples (preferably Granny Smith)
- Craft sticks
- Baking soda
- Table salt
- Quart-size storage bags

Enrichment Reading

Pharaoh's Boat by David L. Weitzman

Mummies Made in Egypt by Aliki

Pyramid, a PBS documentary film or book by David Macaulay

Unit Schedule

Day 1 Discover	Day 2 Explore	Day 3 Create	Day 4 Demonstrate	Day 5 Enrich
UEWH pages 114–117	History Hop! The Chief Embalmer	Make an Apple Mummy	Review Terms & Concepts	Explore Pandia Web Links
HQ Chapter 5 Egypt: Part One	History Travel Log		Complete one or more review options	Read from Enrichment Reading list

Terms & Concepts

The Big Ideas

- Ancient Egyptian civilization began about 5,000 years ago.
- Most of Egypt is made up of desert, but the Nile River flows through it and provides water.
- Egyptians invented a form of writing called hieroglyphics. Hieroglyphics uses pictures, or hieroglyphs, to represent different things, ideas, or even sounds.
- Ancient Egyptians worshipped many gods. Ra, the sun god, was their chief god.
- Egyptians believed that people could live after death if they were good people in life and if their bodies were properly preserved, or mummified.
- Egyptians invented a form of paper known as papyrus, made from reeds that grew along the Nile.
- Egyptians built the Great Pyramid. It still exists today in the city of Giza, and it was built as a special tomb for the pharaoh Khufu.

The Details

- At the very beginning of Egyptian civilization, Upper Egypt and Lower Egypt were unified under the pharaoh Menes.
- Egyptians put tools and riches into pharaohs' tombs so they would have everything they needed to make life comfortable when they moved on to the afterlife.
- The only pharaoh whose tomb was never plundered was Tutankhamun, also known as King Tut. An archaeologist named Howard Carter discovered King Tut's tomb in 1923. Tut's mummy and treasures are now in museums.

Lessons

Day 1. Discover

- ☐ **Read pages 114–117 in UEWH.** If desired, navigate to some of the websites recommended in the book.
- ☐ **Read Chapter 5: Egypt: Part One in HQ pages 63–73**
  ** Refer to the end of this unit for an authors' note about the reading this week.*

Day 2. Explore

- ☐ **Read History Hop! The Chief Embalmer in HQ pages 74–81**
- ☐ **History Travel Log.** Complete the travel log page for this unit and place it in your history notebook.

Day 3. Create

- ☐ **Craft: Make an Apple Mummy**

Supplies:

- Several firm apples, preferably Granny Smith
- Craft sticks
- 2 cups baking soda per apple to be mummified
- 1 cup table salt per apple to be mummified
- Quart-size storage bags, one per apple to be mummified

Directions:

If desired, partially core out the center of the apple through the top. This could approximate removing the "brain" of your apple. Peeling the apple first makes the carving much easier. Using a craft stick, carve a face into your apple. The simplest "face" would be to carve out the spaces for two eyes and a mouth. More sophisticated carvers could carve out the details around the eyes, the mouth, and even a nose, leaving those features raised and prominent. Have several apples on hand in case you need a few attempts to get one the way you want it. Next, stick your craft stick into the top of the apple, to be used as a handle. For each apple to be mummified, mix the baking soda with the table salt. Then place your apple into the bag and make sure it is fully covered by the salt mixture. Place the bag someplace away from high humidity where it will not be disturbed, open at the top. Leave for one week. Finally, remove your mummy from the salt mixture. Gently wipe off the excess mixture with a damp towel and let your mummy air-dry. You might be surprised by the mummy's spongy texture!

Day 4. Demonstrate

☐ **Read through the Terms & Concepts.** Optional: Copy some or all of the Terms & Concepts into your history notebook.

☐ **Complete one or more of the following** in order to strengthen your child's knowledge of the material and to provide an opportunity for you to evaluate their understanding:

Option #1 Short Answers

Answer the following questions verbally or write them in your history notebook:

Q: Why was the southern part of Egypt called Upper Egypt and the northern part of Egypt called Lower Egypt?

A: *The Nile River flows from south to north, so the upstream part of the river is actually in the south.*

Q: Why was the Nile River so important to the ancient Egyptians?

A: *The river flooded every year, making the soil fertile for farming.*

Q: Why did Egyptians build pyramids and mummify their pharaohs?

A: *They believed the pharaoh would go on to an afterlife and that he would need his body and his valuables in order to have a good afterlife.*

Q: What are the names of the type of paper and type of writing that the Egyptians invented?

A: *Their paper is called papyrus, and their writing is called hieroglyphics.*

Q: Pretend you believed the same things the ancient Egyptians believed about the afterlife but you live in your present time. What things would you want to have in your tomb to take to the Field of Reeds?

A: *Answers may vary, but be sure to remind your child if they plan to bring a tablet or smartphone, they should also bring a charging cable!*

Option #2 Narration

Answer the following verbally or in writing:

- List three important things you learned about Ancient Egypt.

Option #3 Copywork/Dictation

Copy or write from dictation one of the following into your history notebook:

The Egyptians invented papyrus, built pyramids, and made mummies.

The ancient Egyptians had a long, peaceful civilization because the Nile River provided what they needed to grow food and the surrounding desert protected them from most invaders. They had writing called hieroglyphics. They invented a kind of paper called papyrus. They built amazing pyramids and also made mummies.

Day 5. Enrich

☐ **Visit www.pandiapress.com/weblinks.** There you will find a description of some recommended websites related to this unit.

☐ **Read one or more from the Enrichment Reading list**

Pharaoh's Boat by David L. Weitzman. Tells about the making, discovery, and recreation of Khufu's (Cheops in the book) boat that was buried with him. Includes a nice pull out showing the scaled length of the boat.

Mummies Made in Egypt by Aliki. Only Aliki could turn a book about mummies into something beautiful. Full of great information and no scary mummy photos for the squeamish. Highly recommended.

Pyramid, a PBS documentary film or book by David Macaulay. An hour-long film intersperses cartoons about Khufu and his Great Pyramid with traditional documentary-style content. You might be able to stream this film, but if not, it should be available through most interlibrary loan systems. Also comes in book form. Macaulay is a master at presenting complicated architectural topics in a way that is accessible and engaging to children. Highly recommended.

Unit Notes

Authors' note about this week's reading:

Ancient Egyptian history spans thousands of years. For our purposes, only a few key issues can be touched upon in this chapter and the next. Because of time constraints, this curriculum won't directly address Egyptian relations with its neighbors, developments, and individuals that came after the New Kingdom era (such as the famous Cleopatra), and many other topics. If your student seems particularly fascinated by ancient Egypt, by all means, look for more material after you finish Units 5 and 6.

The History Quest *chapter provides a general overview of Egyptian history, including reference to the divisions of Old Kingdom, First Intermediate Period, Middle Kingdom, Second Intermediate Period, and New Kingdom. The focus, however, is on Old Kingdom developments. However, the History Hop about the embalmer jumps forward to the New Kingdom. The reason for this is because it wasn't until this period that Egyptians really nailed the process of mummification, and it made sense to teach children about the process once it had reached its maturity. Besides, it gives students a chance to learn about King Tut, the movement of pharaohs to the Valley of the Kings, and the events leading to King Tut's discovery by Howard Carter in 1923.*

UNIT 6

EGYPT: PART TWO

This Week's Quest

Learn about some of Egypt's most famous pharaohs, how they made their marks, and how they sometimes tried to erase the marks of previous pharaohs.

Resources & Materials

History Quest: Early Times (HQ)

Usborne Encyclopedia of World History with Internet Links (UEWH)

Map 2 (Appendix C)

History Travel Log page and The Pharaoh illustration (Appendix C)

Egyptian Hieroglyphs (Appendix C)

Cartouche Template (Appendix C)

Supplies Needed for Day 3

- Coloring tools
- Paper
- Scissors and glue (optional)

Enrichment Reading

Seeker of Knowledge: The Man Who Deciphered Egyptian Hieroglyphs by James Rumford

Horrible Histories: The Awesome Egyptians by Terry Deary and Peter Hepplewhite

DK Eyewitness Books: Ancient Egypt by George Hart

The Shipwrecked Sailor: An Egyptian Tale with Hieroglyphs by Tamara Bower

How the Amazon Queen Fought the Prince of Egypt by Tamara Bower

Unit Schedule

Day 1 Discover	Day 2 Explore	Day 3 Create	Day 4 Demonstrate	Day 5 Enrich
UEWH pages 134–139	History Hop! The Pharaoh	Make Your Own Cartouche	Review Terms & Concepts	Explore Pandia Web Links
HQ Chapter 6 Egypt: Part Two	Google Earth		Complete one or more review options	Read from Enrichment Reading list
Map 2	History Travel Log			

Terms & Concepts

The Big Ideas

- Ahmose was a pharaoh who conquered the Hyksos people—who had taken control of Egypt—and kicked them out.
- Akhenaten was a pharaoh who tried to make all Egyptians worship one god. Once he died, they went back to believing in all their gods.
- Ramses II was the popular pharaoh known as Ramses the Great. He made Egypt even stronger and wealthier than it was before.
- The pharaoh Hatshepsut was a woman who ruled during the New Kingdom. Hatshepsut was a very good ruler. She put many people to work building beautiful buildings and improved trade with foreign people.

The Details

- A person who studies ancient Egypt is an Egyptologist.
- Pharaohs' names were written in a special way. The hieroglyphics of their names were surrounded by an oval. This is called a *cartouche*.

Lessons

Day 1. Discover

- ☐ **Read pages 134–139 in UEWH.** If desired, navigate to some of the websites recommended in the book.
- ☐ **Read Chapter 6: Egypt: Part Two in HQ pages 83–92**
  ** Refer to the end of this unit for an authors' note about the reading this week.*
- ☐ **Complete Map 2.** Referring to the map in HQ on page 82 add the following labels:
  1. Label this body of water:
     Persian Gulf
  2. Label this city:
     •Thebes
  3. Label the area of the Hittite Empire and Mesopotamia.
  4. Shade the Egyptian Empire as of 1500 BCE.

Day 2. Explore

- ☐ **Read History Hop! The Pharaoh in HQ pages 93–100**
- ☐ **Google Earth.** Search for "Giza Necropolis" to check out the pyramids and the Sphinx.
- ☐ **History Travel Log.** Complete the travel log page for this unit and place it in your history notebook.

Day 3. Create

- ☐ **Craft: Make Your Own Cartouche**

Supplies:

- Egyptian Hieroglyphs (Appendix C)
- Cartouche Template (Appendix C)
- Coloring tools—markers, colored pencils, etc.
- Extra paper
- Optional: scissors and glue

Directions:

On a blank sheet of paper, have your child write out their name, leaving big spaces between each letter. Then find the hieroglyph that corresponds with each letter of the name. Either copy each hieroglyph under its corresponding letter, or cut out the hieroglyph from the chart and lay it under each letter. If you choose to do the latter, note that you might need more than one copy of the chart if your child's name has repeated letters. In addition, your child may want to color the hieroglyphs, and if that is the case, it would be better if they colored them in before cutting.

Once you know which hieroglyphs you want to use, decide whether you want to set them into the cartouche horizontally or vertically. Point out that Egyptians presented their names either way. If you have the cut-out (and colored-in) hieroglyphs, glue them onto the cartouche template in proper order. If your child copied the hieroglyphs by hand, direct them to draw them again in the cartouche. Encourage artistic flair with the colors they choose for the hieroglyphs.

Optional: If your child enjoys using the hieroglyphs, you can have them write or decode secret messages using hieroglyphs.

Day 4. Demonstrate

- ☐ **Read through the Terms & Concepts.** Optional: Copy some or all of the Terms & Concepts into your history notebook.
- ☐ **Complete one or more of the following** in order to strengthen your child's knowledge of the material and to provide an opportunity for you to evaluate their understanding:

Option #1 Short Answers

Answer the following questions verbally or write them in your history notebook:

Q: The first pharaoh in the New Kingdom was named Ahmose. What was he able to do for the Egyptians?

A: *Ahmose beat the Hyksos people and kicked them out of Egypt.*

Q: What did the pharaoh Akhenaten believe and how did the other Egyptians feel about this?

A: *Akhenaten made all Egyptians worship one god. After he died, they went back to believing in all their gods.*

Q: Why did people give Ramses II the nickname "Great"? What kind of leader should a person be to deserve that nickname?

A: *Ramses made Egypt even stronger and wealthier than it was before. Answers about the leadership qualities part of the question will vary.*

Q: How was Hatshepsut a good pharaoh? If she was such a good pharaoh, why do you think the next pharaoh, who was her stepson, tried to erase her legacy?

A: Hatshepsut put many people to work building beautiful buildings and improved trade. Answers will vary about why her stepson might have tried to erase her legacy, but one possible reason is because she was such a powerful woman.

Option #2 Narration

Answer the following verbally or in writing:

- List three important things you learned about Egyptian pharaohs.

Option #3 Copywork

Copy or write from dictation one of the following into your history notebook:

Ahmose, Akhenaten, Hatshepsut, and Ramses II were famous pharaohs in Egypt.

The New Kingdom in Egypt began when Ahmose kicked out the foreigners called the Hyksos. Akhenaten was the pharaoh who tried to make the Egyptians worship one god. Hatshepsut was a female pharaoh. Ramses II was called Ramses the Great because he helped Egypt get even stronger and richer than it already was.

Day 5. Enrich

☐ **Visit www.pandiapress.com/weblinks.** There you will find a description of some recommended websites related to this unit.

☐ **Read one or more from the Enrichment Reading list**

Seeker of Knowledge: The Man Who Deciphered Egyptian Hieroglyphs by James Rumford. Beautifully illustrated, well-written story about Jean-Francois Champollion, who figured out how to read Egyptian hieroglyphs in the time of Napoleon. Extra information is included on hieroglyphs themselves scattered through the book and after the story.

Horrible Histories: The Awesome Egyptians by Terry Deary and Peter Hepplewhite. The quirky but historically sophisticated team at *Horrible Histories* has a great entry here with *The Awesome Egyptians*. Proceed with care, though. The type of humor and willingness to discuss the gorier and earthier elements of human reality might not appeal to all parents/teachers and might not be appropriate for all students. If you like *Horrible Histories*, keep in mind that there are many books and videos produced by the group. Perfect for families that appreciate dark humor—not intended for highly sensitive children.

DK Eyewitness Books: Ancient Egypt by George Hart. Typical *DK Eyewitness* book, full of wonderful photos and information.

The Shipwrecked Sailor: An Egyptian Tale with Hieroglyphs by Tamara Bower Excellently illustrated (in Egyptian style) version of an actual ancient Egyptian tale. Extra information about hieroglyphs incorporated both in the story and in an index. Highly recommended.

How the Amazon Queen Fought the Prince of Egypt by Tamara Bower. Another excellent offering from Tamara Bower, this book tells the story of an Egyptian tale with influence from the Greco-Roman period, about the queen of an all-female society who fights against an Egyptian prince. Just like in *The Shipwrecked Sailor*, Bower provides a wealth of information about hieroglyphs.

Unit Notes

Authors' note about this week's reading:

For a variety of reasons, the vast majority of ancient history focuses on men and not very much on women. The same is the case for ancient Egypt, although it seems that, of all the ancient civilizations, women served in more directly influential roles more frequently and generally had more civil protections and rights than in other ancient civilizations. However, it is also the case that sometimes historians who want to counter the bias present in historical writing overestimate the importance of a particular woman in the past. History Quest *strives to strike the appropriate balance with Hatshepsut. Hatshepsut really was far more than simply the "token female" pharaoh. She was a powerful, interesting pharaoh in her own right. But there is not enough corroborating evidence to support some of her own grander claims for her accomplishments, such as leading soldiers in military battle. Thus, this is included in the reading as merely a claim on Hatshepsut's part, not a verified fact.*

Speaking of Hatshepsut, recently, her mummy has been identified by top Egyptologists. Archaeologists already had in their possession a tooth that they knew belonged to Hatshepsut. Like many Egyptians, Hatshepsut suffered from dental problems. Working with a previously unidentified female mummy discovered in the Valley of the Kings, scientists were able to verify that the mummy, conveniently missing a tooth in just the right place, was indeed Hatshepsut. A Google search for "Hatshepsut mummy" will bring up several articles, pictures, and videos about this important archaeological find for those who are interested.

UNIT 7

ANDES MOUNTAIN CIVILIZATIONS

This Week's Quest

Learn about ancient life in the Andes Mountains of South America, where people made very large, beautiful drawings in the desert land.

Resources & Materials

History Quest: Early Times (HQ)

Usborne Encyclopedia of World History with Internet Links (UEWH)

Map 3 (Appendix C)

History Travel Log page and The Potter and the Weaver illustration (Appendix C)

Stirrup Pot coloring pages (Appendix C)

Condor Nazca Line coloring page (Appendix C)

Supplies Needed for Day 3

- Paints and paintbrushes or other coloring tools
- Pencil

Enrichment Reading

Spotlight on Peru by Robin Johnson and Bobbie Kalman

The Llama's Secret: A Peruvian Legend by Argentina Palacios

Alpacas by Michelle Hasselius

Unit Schedule

Day 1 Discover	Day 2 Explore	Day 3 Create	Day 4 Demonstrate	Day 5 Enrich
UEWH page 178	History Hop! The Potter and the Weaver	Color a Nazca Pot and Trace the Nazca Line Condor	Review Terms & Concepts	Explore Pandia Web Links
HQ Chapter 7 Andes Mountain Civilizations	Google Earth		Complete one or more review options	Read from Enrichment Reading list
Map 3	History Travel Log			

Terms & Concepts

The Big Ideas

❋ One of the very oldest civilizations started in South America, in the present-day country of Peru. This civilization is sometimes called the Andean Civilization because it grew up in and around the Andes Mountains.

❋ The Nazca people lived in the Andes 2,000 years ago. They are famous for their large drawings in the desert, their beautiful pottery, and the colorful cloth they weaved.

❋ The people of the ancient Andes had no written language.

The Details

❋ The people of the ancient Andes built pyramids that looked a little like the ziggurats of ancient Mesopotamia.

❋ People in South America domesticated llamas and alpacas, two animals that were like camels. They could be used for carrying things and for their fur.

❋ El Niño is something that happens in the climate near South America from time to time that sometimes brings very bad floods. This affected how the Andean civilization developed.

❋ The people of the ancient Andes probably believed that dead people's spirits could either help or hurt living people. They carefully mummified their friends, and they cut off the heads of their dead enemies.

Lessons

Day 1. Discover

☐ **Read page 178 in UEWH.** If desired, navigate to some of the websites recommended in the book.

☐ **Read Chapter 7: Andes Mountain Civilizations in HQ pages 101–109**
** Refer to the end of this unit for an authors' note about the reading this week.*

☐ **Complete Map 3.** Referring to the map in HQ on page 103 add the following labels:

1. Trace the Amazon River blue, and label these bodies of water:

   Pacific Ocean
   Amazon River

2. Label the locations of these modern-day countries (put in brackets, if desired):

   ECUADOR
   PERU
   COLOMBIA
   BRAZIL
   BOLIVIA

3. Shade the area of the ancient Nazca civilization.

4. Draw triangles to indicate the Andes Mountains.

Day 2. Explore

☐ **Read History Hop! The Potter and the Weaver in HQ pages 110–122**
**Day 3's Nazca Line tracing activity could be completed while reading this unit's History Hop aloud.*

☐ **Google Earth.** Search for "Nazca Lines" and click on the link to see some of this artwork from above.

☐ **History Travel Log.** Complete the travel log page for this unit and place it in your history notebook.

Day 3. Create

☐ **Craft: Color a Nazca Pot and Trace the Nazca Line Condor**

Supplies:

- Stirrup Pot coloring pages (Appendix C)
- Paints (especially black, brown, orange, and red) and paintbrushes, or other coloring tools
- Internet access
- Condor Nazca Line coloring page (Appendix C)
- Pencil

Directions:

Have your child either design their own artwork for the pot or choose colors for the bird design version of the coloring page.

To encourage your child to make their artwork look like a typical Nazca pot, look for pictures of actual Nazca pots to use as examples. Google Images has many to choose from, or you can use a book from the library. It is advisable to review the Google Images search results prior to showing the pictures to your children. While some of the Nazca pottery could be rated "PG-13" for violence, pottery from the Moche people (a later group whose pottery could potentially show up in a search result) has quite a bit of "R-rated" content!

An alternative craft to consider: There are a number of weaving crafts designed for children available for purchase. If your child enjoys crafts like this, you might want to consider getting one. Look for one that approximates a backstrap loom.

In this unit's History Hop reading you fly over Nazca Lines, enormous shapes created by the ancient Andeans. Each was drawn with one continuous, non-intersecting line scratched into the ground of the Nazca desert. The Condor Nazca Line coloring page depicts the Andean condor, one of the world's largest flying birds. Appropriately, the condor Nazca Line is the largest at 440 feet wide—80 feet longer than a football field! Place your pencil somewhere along the dotted line of the condor. Trace the condor in one continuous line. For an added challenge, try tracing without picking up your pencil! Color or paint the condor, if desired.

Day 4. Demonstrate

☐ **Read through the Terms & Concepts.** Optional: Copy some or all of the Terms & Concepts into your history notebook.

☐ **Complete one or more of the following** in order to strengthen your child's knowledge of the material and to provide an opportunity for you to evaluate their understanding:

Option #1 Short Answers

Answer the following questions verbally or write them in your history notebook:

Q: What did the Nazca people make in the desert that still exists today?

A: *They made large line drawings in the desert.*

Q: What kinds of animals did the people of the Andean civilization domesticate?

A: *They domesticated llamas and alpacas.*

Q: How did the people of the ancient Andes feel about their friends and enemies after they died?

A: *They believed that dead people's spirits could either help or hurt living people. They mummified their friends and cut off the heads of their dead enemies.*

Option #2 Narration

Answer the following verbally or in writing:

- List three important things you learned about ancient Andean civilization.

Option #3 Copywork

Copy or write from dictation one of the following into your history notebook:

The ancient Nazca people lived in the Andes, where they made beautiful pottery, clothing, and line drawings in the desert.

A civilization grew thousands of years ago in the Andes Mountains of South America. It had llamas and alpacas. The people of the Andes lived for a long time without fighting but then began to fight a lot. One of the groups was called the Nazca people. They made beautiful pots and clothes. They also drew very long lines and made big pictures in the desert.

Day 5. Enrich

☐ **Visit www.pandiapress.com/weblinks.** There you will find a description of some recommended websites related to this unit.

☐ **Read one or more from the Enrichment Reading list**

Spotlight on Peru by Robin Johnson and Bobbie Kalman. Filled with excellent photographs and a solid overview of all different aspects of Peruvian life, art, and culture, showing the connections between ancient origins and present day. Highly recommended.

The Llama's Secret: A Peruvian Legend by Argentina Palacios. Featuring simple, bold illustrations and pleasant storytelling, *The Llama's Secret* is a retelling of an old South American flood epic.

Alpacas by Michelle Hasselius. A simple book with engaging photographs about an animal group very important to Peruvians, ancient and present. The text is simple enough that many elementary students will be able to read it independently.

Unit Notes

Authors' note about this week's reading:

Communicating the history of the people who lived in and around the Andes Mountains in ancient times is very difficult for a number of reasons. There is much that historians still don't know. There is also a lot of debate among archaeologists about the meaning of different finds. The ancient history of this region is also quite complex, as groups rose and fell in different places, sometimes maintaining certain cultural features from before, sometimes adopting new ones.

When many people think about ancient South American culture, they think about the Inca, a civilization that flourished during medieval times. However, there were many groups in this region who preceded the Inca, so the History Quest *curriculum focuses on some of these groups.*

UNIT 8

MESOAMERICA

This Week's Quest

Learn about civilizations that lived long ago in the land where Mexico is now located.

Resources & Materials

History Quest: Early Times (HQ)

Usborne Encyclopedia of World History with Internet Links (UEWH)

History Travel Log page and The Hero Twins illustration (Appendix C)

Mayan Animal Glyphs coloring page (Appendix C)

Enrichment Reading

Popol Vuh: A Sacred Book of the Maya by Victor Montejo

The Ancient Maya by Jackie Maloy

Supplies Needed for Day 3

- Coloring tools
- Baker's chocolate
- Honey or vegan sweetener
- Chili powder
- Vanilla extract
- Heating source
- Water

Unit Schedule

Day 1 Discover	Day 2 Explore	Day 3 Create	Day 4 Demonstrate	Day 5 Enrich
UEWH pages 179–181	History Hop! The Hero Twins	Color Mayan Glyphs	Review Terms & Concepts	Explore Pandia Web Links
HQ Chapter 8 Mesoamerica	Google Earth	Try Chocolate the Maya Way!	Complete one or more review options	Read from Enrichment Reading list
	History Travel Log			

Terms & Concepts

The Big Ideas

- Mesoamerica is the part of the world between North America and South America. Mexico is the largest present-day country located where ancient Mesoamerican civilization was.
- The most famous ancient people of Mesoamerica were the Maya. They made many discoveries about math and astronomy and wrote in beautiful hieroglyphics. They also fought each other and performed human sacrifices to their gods.

The Details

- Foods like corn, chocolate, vanilla, peppers, tomatoes, peanuts, and squash all were developed in Mesoamerica.
- Another Mesoamerican group called the Olmec were the first group in the area to have written language. They also built huge sculptures called the Colossal Head Sculptures.
- Mesoamericans were the first to play a group ball game, where teams tried to bounce a large rubber ball off their hips to the other side.
- The Maya are also famous for their calendars. One of their calendars came very, very close to predicting exactly how long a year really is. Another of their calendars lasted millions of days.
- The most important story for the Maya people is called the Popol Vuh [puh-POOL vuh]. It tells their story of how everything was created and it also tells stories of some of their heroes, such as the Hero Twins, Hunahpu and Xbalanque [hu-NAH-poo and sh-bah-LAWN-kay].

Lessons

Day 1. Discover

- ☐ **Read pages 179–181 in UEWH.** If desired, navigate to some of the websites recommended in the book.
- ☐ **Read Chapter 8: Mesoamerica in HQ pages 123–132**

  ** Refer to the end of this unit for an authors' note about the reading this week.*

  *** Day 3's coloring activity could be completed while reading Chapter 8 aloud.*

Day 2. Explore

- ☐ **Read History Hop! The Hero Twins in HQ pages 133–138**
- ☐ **Google Earth.** Type in "Chichen Itza" and click on the image to see Maya ruins.
- ☐ **History Travel Log.** Complete the travel log page for this unit and place it in your history notebook.

Day 3. Create

☐ **Craft: Color Mayan Glyphs**

Supplies:

- Mayan Glyphs coloring page (Appendix C)
- Coloring tools—crayons, colored pencils, and/or markers

Directions:

Have your child color the coloring page, perhaps while you are reading one of the reading assignments aloud. The glyphs are based on those found at one of the most important Maya cities, Palenque.

☐ **Cooking: Try Chocolate the Maya Way!**

Supplies:

- 1 ounce unsweetened (baker's) chocolate, cut into small chunks
- 1 teaspoon to 2 tablespoons honey, depending on how sweet/bitter you can handle the recipe (or substitute a vegan sweetener of your choice)

- Up to 1 tablespoon chili powder, depending on how much spiciness you can tolerate
- ½ teaspoon vanilla extract
- Heat source (double boiler or microwave)
- Water

Directions:

Melt the chocolate, either in a double boiler or in 30-second intervals in the microwave (stirring in between intervals). Stir in the honey, chili powder, and vanilla. Add enough water so that you have a rather thick (but still drinkable) mix. Warning: This will taste nothing like the hot cocoa mix you might be used to!

Day 4. Demonstrate

☐ **Read through the Terms & Concepts.** Optional: Copy some or all of the Terms & Concepts into your history notebook.

☐ **Complete one or more of the following** in order to strengthen your child's knowledge of the material and to provide an opportunity for you to evaluate their understanding:

Option #1 Short Answers

Answer the following questions verbally or write them in your history notebook:

Q: Which two continents is Mesoamerica between? What is the largest modern-day country in Mesoamerica?

A: *Mesoamerica is between North America and South America. Mexico is the largest country in Mesoamerica.*

Q: What was the most famous civilization in Mesoamerica?

A: *The most famous civilization was the Maya civilization.*

Q: What was the Mesoamerican ball game like? What could happen to a team if they lost?

A: *The players had to get a ball through a hoop without using their hands. The losing team might be killed.*

Option #2 Narration

Answer the following verbally or in writing:

- List three important things you learned about the ancient Mesoamerican civilization.

Option #3 Copywork/Dictation

Copy or write from dictation one of the following into your history notebook:

The Maya lived in Mesoamerica. They were experts at math and astronomy.

One of the places where ancient civilization began is Mesoamerica, where corn was first grown. The most famous ancient people here were the Maya. The Maya played a special ball game and were experts at math and astronomy. The Maya also fought each other a lot and sometimes practiced human sacrifice.

Day 5. Enrich

☐ **Visit www.pandiapress.com/weblinks.** There you will find a description of some recommended websites related to this unit.

☐ **Read one or more from the Enrichment Reading list**

Popol Vuh: A Sacred Book of the Maya by Victor Montejo. A fuller but still manageable read-aloud version of the Maya's creation myth, going into much more detail about the exploits of the Hero Twins. Lovely illustrations and lyrical writing. Highly recommended.

The Ancient Maya by Jackie Maloy. This is an excellent overview of Maya culture written in a fun style for children, and it includes plenty of full-color pictures of both art and architecture.

Unit Notes

Authors' note about this week's reading:

You will often see the word Mayan *used to describe not only the language of this Mesoamerican people, but also the people themselves and their culture. Properly speaking, the word* Mayan *refers only to the language, whereas the word* Maya *refers to the people and their culture.*

One of the most fascinating stories concerning the Maya couldn't be included in your History Quest *reading because it begins after ancient times. It has to do with how the Mayan language came to be deciphered. The short version: A Catholic bishop tried to destroy Maya literature, partly due to his desire to see certain Maya practices (like human sacrifice) stamped out. But his attempts to destroy inadvertently led to the Mayan "alphabet" being preserved. The story continues into 20th century debates over whether the Mayan hieroglyphs represented things or sounds (it's actually both). One of the highlights of the story involves Russian soldiers who saved a copy of one of the very few remaining Maya books (called the* Dresden Codex*) that had originally been stored in Germany. All of this material would have been off-topic for* History Quest*, but interested parents may want to explore this topic further and perhaps share the highlights with their children.*

UNIT 9

BABYLON

This Week's Quest

Learn about one of the most well-respected ancient civilizations, and whether it really had hanging gardens . . . or not!

Resources & Materials

History Quest: Early Times (HQ)

Usborne Encyclopedia of World History with Internet Links (UEWH)

History Travel Log page and The Babylonian Royal illustration (Appendix C)

Supplies Needed for Day 3

- Ruler
- Pencil
- Large piece of cardboard/poster board
- Paints and paintbrushes (or markers)

Enrichment Reading

Mesopotamia by Sunita Apte

Unit Schedule

Day 1 Discover	Day 2 Explore	Day 3 Create	Day 4 Demonstrate	Day 5 Enrich
UEWH pages 132–133, 150–151	History Hop! The Babylonian Royal	Paint Your Own Ishtar Gate	Review Terms & Concepts	Explore Pandia Web Links
HQ Chapter 9 Babylon	Google Earth		Complete one or more review options	Read from Enrichment Reading list
	History Travel Log			

Terms & Concepts

The Big Ideas

- The Amorites were a group of people who took over southern Mesopotamia and built up the city of Babylon, which became one of the most important cities in all of Mesopotamia. The most famous Amorite ruler was Hammurabi.
- Hammurabi wrote down a code of laws that everyone in his empire had to follow. We call this "Hammurabi's Code." It had some harsh punishments, but it was meant to make life safer for Babylonians.
- Another group of people who ruled the Babylonian Empire was called the Chaldeans. The most famous Chaldean ruler was Nebuchadnezzar, who built beautiful walls around the city.

The Details

- For a very long time, people believed that Nebuchadnezzar built an amazing garden called the Hanging Gardens of Babylon. However, archaeologist Stephanie Dalley has shown that this is probably wrong. Dr. Dalley believes there was an amazing garden built 100 years earlier in the Assyrian Empire.
- One of the groups able to control the Babylonian Empire for a long time was called the Kassites, famous for their light chariots that could hold more than one soldier at a time.
- The city and culture of Babylon became so admired that even outside conquerors were expected not to destroy anything when they conquered it.

Lessons

Day 1. Discover

- ☐ **Read pages 132–133 and 150–151 in UEWH.** If desired, navigate to some of the websites recommended in the book.
- ☐ **Read Chapter 9: Babylon in HQ pages 139–147**

  ** Refer to the end of this unit for an authors' note about the reading this week.*

Day 2. Explore

- ☐ **Read History Hop! The Babylonian Royal in HQ pages 148–155**
- ☐ **Google Earth.** Search for "Ishtar Gate" to get a closer look.
- ☐ **History Travel Log.** Complete the travel log page for this unit and place it in your history notebook.

Day 3. Create

- ☐ **Craft: Paint Your Own Ishtar Gate**

Supplies:

- Ruler
- Pencil
- Large piece of cardboard. If you don't have cardboard available, you could use poster board, a large piece of paper (e.g. from a roll), or several pieces of paper taped together.
- Paints and paintbrushes and/or markers to decorate the "wall"

Directions:

Before getting started, take another look at the famous Ishtar Gate of Babylon. You can find it illustrated in both *History Quest* and the *Usborne Encyclopedia*, or you can look up images online.

Using the ruler as a straightedge, have your child sketch the outline of the Ishtar Gate on the cardboard/poster board. This will make it easier to know where to paint. To color the gate, first paint the entire gate in a bright blue. Once that dries, you can decorate the gate with golden animals and other designs in gold. One of the animals could be an imaginary animal, made up of different parts of real animals, similar to the Babylonian "dragon."

Detail of the Ishtar Gate showing a Babylonian "dragon."

Day 4. Demonstrate

☐ **Read through the Terms & Concepts.** Optional: Copy some or all of the Terms & Concepts into your history notebook.

☐ **Complete one or more of the following** in order to strengthen your child's knowledge of the material and to provide an opportunity for you to evaluate their understanding:

Option #1 Short Answers

Answer the following questions verbally or write them in your history notebook:

Q: What is Hammurabi most famous for?

A: *Hammurabi wrote down a code of laws that everyone had to follow.*

Q: What do many people think Nebuchadnezzar built that maybe he never did?

A: *People thought he built the Hanging Gardens of Babylon, but it now looks as if these gardens were actually in Assyria.*

Q: What do you think about the laws Hammurabi came up with? Are they fair or unfair? How do we punish people for committing crimes nowadays? What do you think should be the consequence when someone commits a crime?

A: *Answers will vary. This can lead to a fascinating conversation with your child about punitive and restorative justice, depending on your child's level of maturity. Elementary kids tend to be very interested in what's "fair" and "unfair." Feel free to take some time to explore this fascinating topic.*

Option #2 Narration

Answer the following verbally or in writing:

- List three important things you learned about Babylonian civilization.

Option #3 Copywork/Dictation

Copy or write from dictation one of the following into your history notebook:

Babylon was one of the most important cities in Mesopotamia. Two of its rulers were Hammurabi and Nebuchadnezzar.

The city of Babylon was one of the most important cities in ancient Mesopotamia. Many groups ruled it at different times. Hammurabi was a ruler who made a code of laws. Nebuchadnezzar was another ruler who made the Babylonian Empire strong.

Day 5. Enrich

☐ **Visit www.pandiapress.com/weblinks.** There you will find a description of some recommended websites related to this unit.

☐ **Read from the Enrichment Reading list**

Mesopotamia by Sunita Apte. This book covers several Mesopotamian societies, not just Babylon, but includes nice photos of part of the Ishtar Gate, plus an artistic rendering of what the Hanging Gardens of Babylon might have looked like. This is also a good book to have around for the unit on Assyria.

Unit Notes

Authors' note about this week's reading:

For much of ancient history, Babylon (the city and the extended empire) was ruled by non-Babylonians, such as the Akkadians, Hittites, Assyrians, and Chaldeans. To avoid overloading this unit with too much detail, History Quest *focuses on the culture and city of Babylon itself.*

Hammurabi and Nebuchadnezzar, arguably Babylon's most famous leaders, came from different groups and lived more than a thousand years apart. These two had little in common. However, the city of Babylon was vital to both, and both of them are important to understanding ancient history.

Recent research suggests that the Hanging Gardens were actually located in Assyria, not Babylon. However, this is a new finding, and students continuing their studies in ancient history with other resources besides History Quest *(such as the* UEWH *reading) will likely still hear about the "Hanging Gardens of Babylon," built by Nebuchadnezzar.*

UNIT 10

ASSYRIA

This Week's Quest

Learn about a fierce group of people famous for their iron weapons, horses and chariots, and their library.

Resources & Materials

History Quest: Early Times (HQ)

Usborne Encyclopedia of World History with Internet Links (UEWH)

History Travel Log page and The Ironworker illustration (Appendix C)

Note: Unfortunately, there aren't any readily available books about ancient Assyria that are targeted toward elementary-age students.

Supplies Needed for Day 3

- Pencil
- Cardboard
- White glue
- Metallic paints
- Paintbrushes

Unit Schedule

Day 1 Discover	Day 2 Explore	Day 3 Create	Day 4 Demonstrate	Day 5 Enrich
UEWH pages 146–149	History Hop! The Ironworker	Make an Assyrian "Metal" Work Plaque	Review Terms & Concepts	Explore Pandia Web Links
HQ Chapter 10 Assyria	History Travel Log		Complete one or more review options	

Terms & Concepts

The Big Ideas

- Assyria, in the northern part of Mesopotamia, was a powerful civilization that conquered both Babylon and Egypt at different times in history.
- The Assyrians were powerful because they made good use of horses and chariots, iron for weapons, siege engines, and a full-time professional army.

The Details

- The Iron Age was the time in history when people started replacing bronze tools and weapons with iron. This started at different times all over the world.
- Famous Assyrian emperors include Shamshi-Adad (Assyria's founder), Sargon II (who destroyed Israel), Sennacherib (who probably built the hanging gardens), and Ashurbanipal (who built a huge library in Nineveh).
- Around 600 BCE, an alliance of outside groups destroyed the Assyrian Empire for good.

Lessons

Day 1. Discover

- ☐ **Read pages 146–149 in UEWH.** If desired, navigate to some of the websites recommended in the book.
- ☐ **Read Chapter 10: Assyria in HQ pages 157–166**

Day 2. Explore

- ☐ **Read History Hop! The Ironworker in HQ pages 167–174**
- ☐ **History Travel Log.** Complete the travel log page for this unit and place it in your history notebook.

Day 3. Create

- ☐ **Craft: Make an Assyrian "Metal" Work Plaque**

Supplies:

- Pencil
- Pieces of cardboard
- White glue in bottle with a small tip (e.g. Elmer's brand)
- Metallic-colored paints, preferably in a few different colors
- Paintbrushes
- Optional: Print out a few pictures of Assyrian art as inspiration. Try a Google Images search for "Assyrian Art Patterns."

Directions:

Pencil your design choice on a piece of cardboard. Once you have it the way you want, trace the pattern with the glue. It might be a good idea to practice tracing straight and curved lines with glue on a regular piece of paper first, since it can be tricky for children (and adults) to do the right amount of squeezing and such. Let the glue dry for several hours, or preferably overnight. When completely dry, paint over the glue with metallic paints.

Day 4. Demonstrate

- ☐ **Read through the Terms & Concepts.** Optional: Copy some or all of the Terms & Concepts into your history notebook.
- ☐ **Complete one or more of the following** in order to strengthen your child's knowledge of the material and to provide an opportunity for you to evaluate their understanding:

Option #1 Short Answers

Answer the following questions verbally or write them in your history notebook:

Q: Describe two reasons why the Assyrians became as strong as they did.

A: *Answers may vary, and might include: The Assyrians made use of horses and chariots, iron for weapons, siege engines, and a full-time professional army.*

Q: What did the Assyrian emperor Ashurbanipal build in the new capital city of Nineveh?

A: *He built a library.*

Q: Which two other civilizations did Assyria conquer?

A: *The Assyrians conquered both Babylon and Egypt.*

Option #2 Narration

Answer the following verbally or in writing:

- List three important things you learned about Assyrian civilization.

Option #3 Copywork/Dictation

Copy or write from dictation one of the following into your history notebook:

> The Assyrians were a strong, fighting people who used horses, chariots, and iron weapons to defeat other people.

The Assyrians were a strong, fighting people who had an empire in ancient Mesopotamia. They used horses, chariots, and iron weapons to defeat other people. One of their emperors started a library to collect everything that was written. We have learned a lot about ancient Mesopotamia because of that library.

Day 5. Enrich

☐ **Visit www.pandiapress.com/weblinks.** There you will find a description of some recommended websites related to this unit.

Unit Notes

UNIT 11

PERSIA

This Week's Quest

Learn about an empire that grew to be the largest of its time, but that still couldn't manage to conquer the Greeks.

Resources & Materials

History Quest: Early Times (HQ)

Usborne Encyclopedia of World History with Internet Links (UEWH)

History Travel Log page and The Ally illustration (Appendix C)

Note: Unfortunately, there aren't any readily available books about the ancient Persians that are targeted toward elementary-age students.

Supplies Needed for Day 3

- Ground meat (or vegetarian equivalent)
- Onion
- Turmeric
- Cinnamon
- Salt
- Oil
- Plain yogurt
- Cucumber

Unit Schedule

Day 1 Discover	Day 2 Explore	Day 3 Create	Day 4 Demonstrate	Day 5 Enrich
UEWH pages 152–153	History Hop! The Ally	Cook a Persian Meal—Koofteh	Review Terms & Concepts	Explore Pandia Web Links
HQ Chapter 11 Persia	Google Earth		Complete one or more review options	Read from Enrichment Reading list
	History Travel Log			

Terms & Concepts

The Big Ideas

- Cyrus the Great founded the Persian Empire, which was the biggest empire in history at that point in time. Cyrus was popular, even among those he conquered.
- The emperor Darius made the Persian Empire even stronger and larger. But when he tried to conquer the Greeks, they beat him at the Battle of Marathon.

The Details

- The Immortals were a group of 10,000 Persian soldiers who were highly trained to do whatever the Persian emperor needed. If one of them died, another soldier quickly took his place.
- Today, people run marathons to celebrate the legendary twenty-six-mile run that a Greek man made between Marathon and his home city of Athens to report the news that the Greeks had beat the Persians.
- A queen named Artemisia led her own troops into the Battle of Salamis, fighting on the Persian side. When she realized the Persians were going to lose, she led her ship into a daring and clever escape, tricking both Greeks and Persians.

Lessons

Day 1. Discover

- ☐ **Read pages 152–153 in UEWH.** If desired, navigate to some of the websites recommended in the book.
- ☐ **Read Chapter 11: Persia in HQ pages 175–183**
  ** Refer to the end of this unit for an authors' note about the reading this week.*

Day 2. Explore

- ☐ **Read History Hop! The Ally in HQ pages 184–192**
- ☐ **Google Earth.** Search for "Marathon" to see the site of this famous battle between the Persians and Greeks.
- ☐ **History Travel Log.** Complete the travel log page for this unit and place it in your history notebook.

Day 3. Create

- ☐ **Craft: Cook a Persian Meal—Koofteh (Persian Meatballs)**

Supplies:

- ½ pound ground protein of your choice (ground beef, turkey, chicken, or for a meatless version, use textured vegetable protein or frozen "crumbles")
- 2 tablespoons grated onion
- ¼ teaspoon turmeric
- ¼ teaspoon cinnamon
- ¼ teaspoon salt
- Oil for frying
- Plain yogurt and sliced cucumbers for serving

The descendants of the ancient Persians live in the present-day country of Iran. You can become a little more familiar with their Persian heritage by making this easy and delicious meal. There are many varieties of Koofteh (also spelled Kofte). This one is adapted from the website MyPersianKitchen.com.

Directions:

Mix the onion, spices, and salt into the ground meat. Form small meatballs. Fry the meatballs in a small amount of oil until lightly browned all over. Add ¼ cup water and a little bit more salt to the pot, cover, and cook for 20 minutes. Serve with plain yogurt and sliced cucumbers.

Day 4. Demonstrate

- ☐ **Read through the Terms & Concepts.** Optional: Copy some or all of the Terms & Concepts into your history notebook.
- ☐ **Complete one or more of the following** in order to strengthen your child's knowledge of the material and to provide an opportunity for you to evaluate their understanding:

Option #1 Short Answers

Answer the following questions verbally or write them in your history notebook:

Q: Who started the Persian Empire, and did people like him or dislike him?
A: Cyrus the Great started the empire. He was very popular.

Q: What did Darius and Xerxes both *try* to do that they both *failed* to do?
A: They both tried to conquer the Greeks, but they couldn't do it.

Q: Who were the Immortals?
A: The Immortals were highly trained soldiers who did what the emperor wanted.

Option #2 Narration

Answer the following verbally or in writing:

- List three important things you learned about the ancient Persian civilization.

Option #3 Copywork/Dictation

Copy or write from dictation one of the following into your history notebook:

Cyrus the Great started the Persian Empire. It was bigger than any empire before it.

The Persians made an empire that was bigger than any other empire before it. It was started by Cyrus the Great. People admired Cyrus because he was a good ruler. The Persians tried to conquer the Greeks but they couldn't do it.

Day 5. Enrich

- ☐ **Visit www.pandiapress.com/weblinks.** There you will find a description of some recommended websites related to this unit.

Unit Notes

Authors' note about this week's reading:

Calling this unit "Persia" is a bit of an oversimplification. The Persians were initially a vassal group to the Medes. The Medes had already conquered some parts of what would become the Persian Empire when Cyrus, a Persian, conquered the Medes.

UNIT 12

HEBREWS AND PHOENICIANS

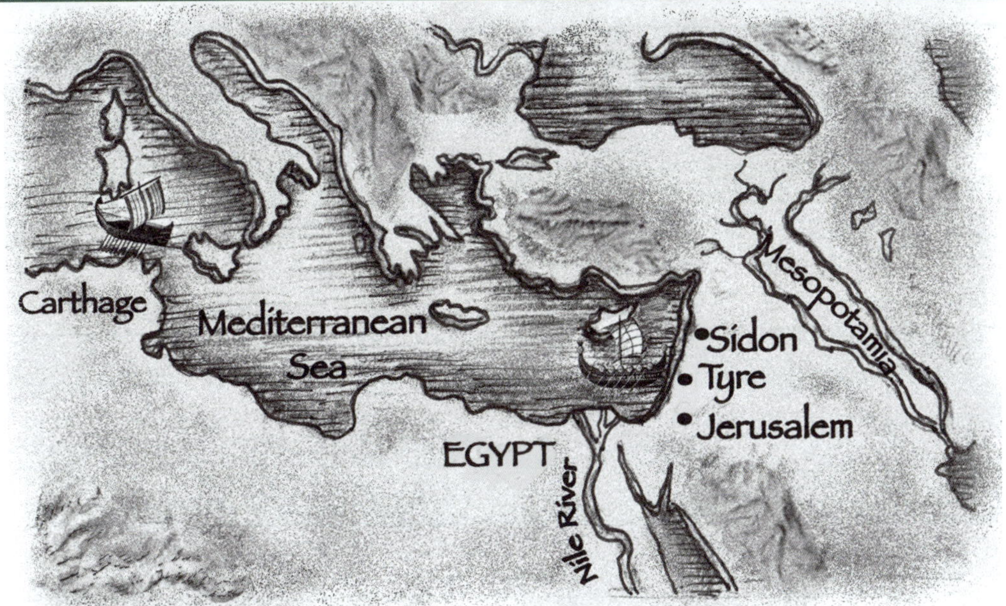

This Week's Quest

Learn about the Hebrews and the Phoenicians, two civilizations that were rather small in size, but that made large impacts on culture.

Resources & Materials

History Quest: Early Times (HQ)

Usborne Encyclopedia of World History with Internet Links (UEWH)

Map 4 (Appendix C)

History Travel Log page and The Sailor illustration (Appendix C)

Supplies Needed for Day 3

- Empty paper towel tubes
- Stuffing such as tissue or newspaper
- Wooden dowels or chopsticks
- Butcher paper or other long paper
- Markers
- Glue

Enrichment Reading

The Usborne Encyclopedia of World Religions by Susan Meredith

Unit Schedule

Day 1 Discover	Day 2 Explore	Day 3 Create	Day 4 Demonstrate	Day 5 Enrich
UEWH pages 142–145	History Hop! The Sailor	Design Your Own Hebrew Scroll	Review Terms & Concepts	Explore Pandia Web Links
HQ Chapter 12 Hebrews and Phoenicians	Google Earth		Complete one or more review options	Read from Enrichment Reading list
Map 4	History Travel Log			

Terms & Concepts

The Big Ideas

❋ The Hebrews, also known as the Israelites or Jews, believed in one god, unlike most other ancient groups, who believed in many gods. They wrote about their beliefs in the Old Testament of the Bible.

❋ The Phoenicians, also known as Canaanites, were experts at shipbuilding and sailing. They used their sailing skills to become wealthy merchants.

❋ The Phoenicians also developed a new way of writing—an alphabet made up of letters that build words, rather than using a different picture for every word.

The Details

❋ The Hebrews split their kingdom around the year 930 BCE, and became two different kingdoms called Israel and Judah.

❋ The Assyrians conquered Israel in 722 BCE and scattered the Israelites. The Babylonians conquered Judah around 587 BCE and exiled many of the Hebrews. But when the Persian emperor Cyrus came to power, he allowed the Jews to move back to their homeland.

❋ The Phoenicians were also famous for making a purple dye for fabric that people all around them loved.

Lessons

Day 1. Discover

- ☐ **Read pages 142–145 in UEWH.** If desired, navigate to some of the websites recommended in the book.
- ☐ **Read Chapter 12: Hebrews and Phoenicians in HQ pages 193–200**
- ☐ **Complete Map 4.** Referring to the map in HQ on page 193 add the following labels:
  1. Label these bodies of water:

     Mediterranean Sea

     Nile River
  2. Label these cities:

     •Carthage

     •Sidon

     •Tyre

     •Jerusalem
  3. Label the country:

     EGYPT
  4. Label this area:

     Mesopotamia

Day 2. Explore

- ☐ **Read History Hop! The Sailor in HQ pages 201–210**
- ☐ **Google Earth.** Search for "Mediterranean Sea." You will get a nice overhead view of where the Phoenicians sailed.
- ☐ **History Travel Log.** Complete the travel log page for this unit and place it in your history notebook.

Day 3. Create

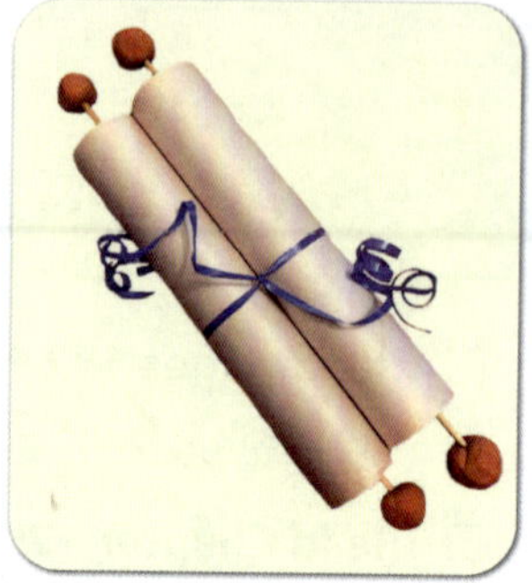

☐ **Craft: Design Your Own Hebrew Scroll**

Supplies:

- 2 empty paper towel tubes (can be cut to size if needed)
- Tissue paper, plastic wrap, newspaper, or other material that can be balled up and stuffed inside the paper towel rolls
- 2 wooden dowels cut to size (chopsticks or skewers will work as well)
- Brown butcher paper, paper from a roll of children's drawing paper, or construction paper
- Glue
- Optional: markers, wooden or clay balls, ribbon

Directions:

Insert a wooden dowel or chopstick into each paper towel tube. Make sure that there is at least an inch of the wood sticking out on both ends of the tube. Cut the sticks or the paper towel tubes to size as necessary. Stuff tissue paper, newspaper, or whatever other material you can use into the paper towel tubes to keep the wooden sticks in place in the middle of each tube.

Measure a piece of paper so that it is the same width as, or even a little narrower than, the paper towel tubes. The length can vary, depending on how thick you want your scrolls. You could cut a long piece from a roll of children's art paper, or even tape together multiple pieces of construction paper. You can also use other material besides paper for the parchment. Felt is a possibility, but writing a message on felt can be difficult.

If desired, encourage your child to write a message on the center of the scroll. One option is to search online for Hebrew writing and copy an appropriate short phrase or word in Hebrew (right to left) on the scroll before rolling it up. Another suggestion is to find an online image for the Hebrew word *shalom* (peace) and copy that.

Glue the edges of the paper to each of the paper towel rolls, allow time to dry, and then roll them toward each other until you have formed your scroll. If your scroll has a tendency to want to unroll itself, you can always tie it together with a decorative ribbon.

If desired, make your scroll even fancier by gluing wooden or clay balls to the ends of the dowels. You can paint the wooden dowels and wooden balls to give your scroll a more finished appearance.

Day 4. Demonstrate

- ☐ **Read through the Terms & Concepts.** Optional: Copy some or all of the Terms & Concepts into your history notebook.
- ☐ **Complete one or more of the following** in order to strengthen your child's knowledge of the material and to provide an opportunity for you to evaluate their understanding:

Option #1 Short Answers

Answer the following questions verbally or write them in your history notebook:

Q: How many gods did the Hebrews believe in? Why was this different than other groups in ancient times?

A: *They believed in one god. Most other ancient groups believed in many gods.*

Q: What were the Phoenicians good at?

A: *They were good at sailing and trading.*

Q: What did the Phoenicians invent that we still use today?

A: *They invented the alphabet.*

Option #2 Narration

Answer the following verbally or in writing:

- List three important things you learned about ancient Hebrew and Phoenician civilizations.

Option #3 Copywork

Copy or write from dictation one of the following into your history notebook:

> The Phoenicians were good at sailing and they invented the alphabet.

The Hebrews were a small group of people who were different from the other ancient groups because they believed in only one god. The Phoenicians were a small group of people who became very wealthy because they became merchants. They were very good at sailing and starting colonies.

Day 5. Enrich

☐ **Read from the Enrichment Reading list**

We typically include a list of additional books here related to the civilizations being studied, but in this case, we were not able to find readily available, age-appropriate books that meet our definition of secular. For those interested in learning more about various world religions (including Judaism, which is covered in this unit), this may be a good time to read *The Usborne Encyclopedia of World Religions* by Susan Meredith. As always, we recommend reviewing this resource ahead of time to make sure you find it appropriate for your child.

Unit Notes

UNIT 13

MINOANS AND MYCENAEANS

This Week's Quest

Learn about how civilization started in Greece with the Minoans and Mycenaeans, and meet one of ancient literature's cleverest heroes.

Resources & Materials

History Quest: Early Times (HQ)

Usborne Encyclopedia of World History with Internet Links (UEWH)

History Travel Log page and The Legend illustration (Appendix C)

Minoan Pottery and Cyclops coloring pages (Appendix C)

Enrichment Reading

You Wouldn't Want to Be a Greek Athlete! by Michael Ford

DK Eyewitness Books: Ancient Greece by Anne Pearson

The Wanderings of Odysseus by Rosemary Sutcliff

Supplies Needed for Day 3

- Coloring tools

Unit Schedule

Day 1 Discover	Day 2 Explore	Day 3 Create	Day 4 Demonstrate	Day 5 Enrich
UEWH pages 124–131	History Hop! The Legend	Color Minoan Pottery and Cyclops	Review Terms & Concepts	Explore Pandia Web Links
HQ Chapter 13 Minoans and Mycenaeans	Google Earth		Complete one or more review options	Read from Enrichment Reading list
	History Travel Log			

Terms & Concepts

The Big Ideas

- Ancient Greek civilization started on an island in the middle of the Mediterranean Sea called Crete. The people who began this civilization are called Minoans.
- Minoan civilization weakened after a big wave called a *tsunami* hit Crete around 1600 BCE. By 1400 BCE, the Mycenaeans from nearby Greece took over in both Crete and Greece, starting the Mycenaean civilization.
- The Mycenaean civilization was destroyed during the Bronze Age Collapse around the year 1200 BCE. Soon after, Greece entered its Dark Ages and people stopped writing things down.

The Details

- The Minoans are famous for their strong navy, fresco paintings, cities without walls, and sports such as bull leaping.
- The Mycenaeans had writing and art, but they were much more interested in fighting. They had bronze weapons and chariots.
- During the Greek Dark Ages, people told epics, which were long and exciting stories about heroes. The two most famous Greek epics are the *Iliad* and *Odyssey*.
- One of the heroes of both the *Iliad* and *Odyssey* is Odysseus, who was known for his cleverness. In the *Iliad*, he comes up with the idea to hide soldiers in a giant hollow horse made out of wood.

Lessons

Day 1. Discover

- ☐ **Read pages 124–131 in UEWH.** If desired, navigate to some of the websites recommended in the book.
- ☐ **Read Chapter 13: Minoans and Mycenaeans in HQ pages 211–220**

  ** Refer to the end of this unit for an authors' note about the reading this week.*

Day 2. Explore

- ☐ **Read History Hop! The Legend in HQ pages 221–228**
- ☐ **Google Earth.** Search for "Minoan Palace at Knossos" and click on the image to see inside this archaeological site.
- ☐ **History Travel Log.** Complete the travel log page for this unit and place it in your history notebook.

Day 3. Create

- ☐ **Craft: Color Minoan Pottery and Cyclops**

Supplies:

- Coloring tools: markers, paints, and/or colored pencils
- Minoan Pottery and Cyclops coloring pages (Appendix C)

Directions:

The Minoans loved to depict sea creatures in their beautiful pottery. One famous form of pottery in ancient Greece is the amphora, a rather tall jar with a narrow opening at the top and a handle on each side. This week, your child can either draw and decorate their own amphora, or color/paint a coloring page of a famous piece of Minoan pottery from around 3,500 years ago.

Polyphemus, a one-eyed monster called a cyclops, eats people for lunch in the *Odyssey*. The cyclops coloring page would be a good coloring activity if you're reading *The Wanderings of Odysseus* by Rosemary Sutcliff or another children's version of the *Odyssey*.

Day 4. Demonstrate

☐ **Read through the Terms & Concepts.** Optional: Copy some or all of the Terms & Concepts into your history notebook.

☐ **Complete one or more of the following** in order to strengthen your child's knowledge of the material and to provide an opportunity for you to evaluate their understanding:

Option #1 Short Answers

Answer the following questions verbally or write them in your history notebook:

Q: What were the names of the first two groups that started ancient Greek civilization?
A: *They were the Minoans (first) and the Mycenaeans (second).*

Q: What kind of natural disaster made the Minoans weaker?
A: *A tsunami (a gigantic wave) hit their island.*

Q: During the Greek Dark Ages, what did people do for entertainment?
A: *The told stories such as the* Iliad *and* Odyssey.

Option #2 Narration

Answer the following verbally or in writing:

- List three important things you learned about ancient Greek civilization.

Option #3 Copywork/Dictation

Copy or write from dictation one of the following into your history notebook:

> Ancient Greek civilization started with the Minoans and Mycenaeans.

Ancient Greek civilization started with the Minoans on Crete. They were rich and peaceful. Then a rougher group called the Mycenaeans took over. Then ancient Greece had a Dark Age when everyone stopped writing things down. They began telling epic stories like the Iliad and Odyssey.

Day 5. Enrich

- ☐ **Visit www.pandiapress.com/weblinks.** There you will find a description of some recommended websites related to this unit.
- ☐ **Read one or more from the Enrichment Reading list**

You Wouldn't Want to Be a Greek Athlete! by Michael Ford. Another in the *You Wouldn't Want to Be...* series. This book includes information that is covered by all of *History Quest*'s chapters about Greece, but seemed most appropriate for the first chapter. Parents may want to review the text and pictures of the book before deciding whether or not to use—as Greek Olympians competed in the nude, there are quite a few cartoonish backsides illustrated.

DK Eyewitness Books: Ancient Greece by Anne Pearson. This is a solid overview of ancient Greece starting with the Minoans and running through the time of Alexander the Great. This is a good book to have handy during the next several units.

The Wanderings of Odysseus by Rosemary Sutcliff. Sutcliff's version of the *Odyssey* for younger audiences is a classic. Please note that the *Odyssey* is a sequel to the *Iliad*, but it is not truly necessary to read them in order. Next week's Hygge History unit includes Sutcliff's version of the *Iliad* titled *Black Ships Before Troy*. Both books are highly recommended.

Unit Notes

Authors' note about this week's reading:

The Iliad *and* Odyssey *are often presented as having been written by a Greek man named Homer sometime in the 700s BCE. Historians debate whether such an individual existed. However, the legends were well known by all Greeks for hundreds of years before they were codified. It is difficult to underestimate how important the* Iliad *and* Odyssey *were to the ancient Greek mindset. These Greek epics continue to be retold in various forms through Western history. Two American works that were influenced by the* Odyssey *are Mark Twain's* The Adventures of Huckleberry Finn *and the Coen Brothers movie,* O Brother, Where Art Thou? *(2000).*

HYGGE HISTORY #2

GREEK MYTHOLOGY

This Week's Quest

Read and enjoy classic Greek literature.

Resources

Black Ships Before Troy by Rosemary Sutcliff (ISBN 978-0385310697)

or choose,

D'Aulaires' Book of Greek Myths by Ingri d'Aulaire and Edgar Parin d'Aulaire (ISBN 978-0440406945)

Hygge History

Welcome to your second week of Hygge History, where cozy enjoyment of classic literature is your only assignment. There are no worksheets or assignments to complete. Just read and enjoy.

Here are our two picks:

Option 1: *Black Ships Before Troy*

Black Ships Before Troy is a version of the *Iliad* written for children by Rosemary Sutcliff. In fact, you can even take two weeks if you want to also snuggle up with Sutcliff's version of the *Odyssey*, called *The Wanderings of Odysseus*, if you didn't get a chance to read it during the previous unit. Besides being wonderful retellings of these classic stories, both books are remarkable works of literature in their own right. If you can make the time, do try to read both *Black Ships Before Troy* and *The Wanderings of Odysseus* at some point in your children's lives, even if you can't fit them both in during this school year. Sutcliff's versions of the Homeric legends have been paired with different illustrators, depending on the publisher, but the versions illustrated by Alan Lee (famed illustrator of *The Lord of the Rings* books and Oscar-winning conceptual artist for the movies of those books) are treasures. It is well worth it to get copies of the Alan Lee-illustrated versions of these books!

Black Ships Before Troy tells the story of the *Iliad*, which dates to about the eighth century BCE. As such, readers should expect some problematic portrayals of female characters. Helen's legendary beauty is the cause of the Trojan War, and several of the male characters treat her as an object, pawn, or prize throughout the story. The captive woman, Briseis, fares no better. However, the story does include two strong mythological females: Thetis and Andromache, who are often cited in feminist literary criticisms of the *Iliad*. *Black Ships Before Troy* also devotes an entire chapter to the Amazon warrior Penthesilea, whose war prowess puts a dent in the Greek forces.

Sutcliff's version tells the story of the *Iliad* in novel form (rather than the original epic poem) in nineteen chapters. It is not a book you will be able to read aloud in one sitting. Consider your child's attention span when reading. You might be able to get through one, two, or three chapters in a sitting. Don't push it, trying to squeeze in just one more chapter. The language is rich and the story is dramatic and suspenseful—kids will need a breather between chapters. Some parents have reported success with reading one chapter during daytime schoolwork and a second chapter as a bedtime story; this approach will get you through the book in about ten days.

Take your time and relish the experience of your child's first exposure to the *Iliad*. Stop along the way to discuss both the good choices and terrible mistakes the characters make, as well as the themes of loyalty, pride, friendship, and fate versus free will. And if you do decide to read *The Wanderings of Odysseus* at this time, pay special attention to Odysseus's choices along the way and the consequences he faces as a result. While it's not every day that we have to choose whether to travel dangerously close to a deadly whirlpool or instead face a six-headed monster, we can all identify with Odysseus and the many tough calls he has to make in order to get himself home.

Option 2: *D'Aulaires' Book of Greek Myths*

If you are short on time, or if you determine that *Black Ships Before Troy* is not a good match for your child's attention, interest, or maturity, take a look at *D'Aulaires' Book of Greek Myths* by Ingri d'Aulaire and Edgar Parin d'Aulaire. There are many collections of ancient Greek myths, but the d'Aulaires' version has to be the definitive one. A good collection of Greek myths should be part of every child's education, even if you find you don't have time to include it in this school year's studies.

UNIT 14

GREECE DEVELOPS

This Week's Quest

Learn about an ancient Greek civilization known for its tough citizens and no-nonsense attitude, the Spartans.

Resources & Materials

History Quest: Early Times (HQ)

Usborne Encyclopedia of World History with Internet Links (UEWH)

Map 5 (Appendix C)

History Travel Log page and The Queen illustration (Appendix C)

Supplies Needed for Day 3

- Clay, Model Magic, or similar material (silver color clay or silver paint)
- Pencil or other item for carving

Enrichment Reading

Sports Heroes of Ancient Greece by Paul Mason

The Spartan Hoplites by Louise Park and Timothy Love

Unit Schedule

Day 1 Discover	Day 2 Explore	Day 3 Create	Day 4 Demonstrate	Day 5 Enrich
UEWH pages 154–157	History Hop! The Queen	Make Your Own Owl Coin	Review Terms & Concepts	Explore Pandia Web Links
HQ Chapter 14 Greece Develops	History Travel Log		Complete one or more review options	Read from Enrichment Reading list
Map 5				

Terms & Concepts

The Big Ideas

❋ Greek society was built around the city-state, which was made up of a city center surrounded by farmland. The Greek word for city-state is polis [PAUL-is].

❋ One famous city-state was Sparta. Sparta was famous for its fighting skills, the loyalty of its citizens, and the way the Spartan people didn't try to show off their wealth.

❋ The ancient Greeks started the Olympics, which is a big sporting competition that many countries around the world participate in every four years.

The Details

❋ The ancient Greeks were split from each other because of their geography—hills and mountains kept people apart. The Greeks formed smaller groups instead of one large society.

❋ Sparta had a queen named Gorgo who gave her people good advice about how to keep her city strong. Her husband, King Leonidas, helped the Greeks fight against the Persians.

❋ Most ancient Greek men looked down on women, but women were treated with more respect in Sparta as compared to most other places during ancient times.

Lessons

Day 1. Discover

- ☐ **Read pages 154-157 in UEWH.** If desired, navigate to some of the websites recommended in the book.
- ☐ **Read Chapter 14: Greece Develops in HQ pages 229–239**

  ** Refer to the end of this unit for an authors' note about the reading this week.*
- ☐ **Complete Map 5.** Referring to the map in HQ on page 232 add the following labels:
  1. Label the following:

     GREECE

     Mediterranean Sea

     Mount Olympus
  2. Label these cities:

     •Thebes

     •Sparta

     •Messene

     •Corinth

     •Athens
  3. Add triangles to show the mountainous areas of Greece.

Day 2. Explore

- ☐ **Read History Hop! The Queen in HQ pages 240–248**
- ☐ **History Travel Log.** Complete the travel log page for this unit and place it in your history notebook.

Day 3. Create

☐ **Craft: Make Your Own Owl Coin**

Supplies:

- Clay (or similar material such as Model Magic) preferably silver color (or paint the coin silver after baking)
- Pencil or other tool for carving an image in the clay
- "The Queen" History Travel Log illustration for reference (Appendix C)

Directions:

Take a large piece of clay and flatten it out into a disk. The larger the disk, the easier it will be to add the design. It will be very difficult to create the image if you try to make it as small as the original coin. The coin does not need to be a perfect circle since the Athenian coins were often not perfectly round. Using a pencil or other thin tool, carve the image of the "owl of Athena" onto the top of the disk. Use the picture of the owl coin found on The Queen illustration as a reference, or conduct an online search of "Athenian owl coin" to see many examples. You can simplify the image if it's too challenging. Add the other details to your coin if you wish—the sprig of leaves to the left and the Greek inscription ΑΘΕ on the right. If you want to display the coin, make a hole at the top for a string or hook. When your coin is done, bake according to package instructions (if required for the clay you are using).

Note: ΑΘΕ is an abbreviation for ΑΘΗΝΑΙΩΝ, which means "of the Athenians."

Day 4. Demonstrate

☐ **Read through the Terms & Concepts.** Optional: Copy some or all of the Terms & Concepts into your history notebook.

☐ **Complete one or more of the following** in order to strengthen your child's knowledge of the material and to provide an opportunity for you to evaluate their understanding:

Option #1 Short Answers

Answer the following questions verbally or write them in your history notebook:

Q: What was the name of the city-state in ancient Greece that was famous for its fighting skills?
A: Sparta was famous for its fighting skills.

Q: What sports competition did the ancient Greeks start that we still hold in modern times?

A: *They started the Olympics.*

Q: How were women treated in Sparta compared to other city-states?

A: *Women were treated better in Sparta than in other places in ancient Greece.*

Option #2 Narration

Answer the following verbally or in writing:

- List three important things you learned about early ancient Greek civilization.

Option #3 Copywork

Copy or write from dictation one of the following into your history notebook:

Sparta was a city-state that trained its children to care only about Sparta.

Ancient Greece was divided into many cities. Life in the city of Sparta was hard. Spartan men were trained to fight. Spartan women did not fight, but they were more respected than women in other ancient Greek cities.

Day 5. Enrich

☐ **Read from the Enrichment Reading list**

Sports Heroes of Ancient Greece by Paul Mason. This book balances an overview of the ancient Olympics with spotlights on various actual athletes. Remember, ancient Greeks competed in the nude, but this book's illustrations and photos manage to present the nudity in a way that should not be problematic for most families.

The Spartan Hoplites by Louise Park and Timothy Love. This book digs deeper into the army, government, and school system of Sparta. *Note: Since the book focuses on what it was like to serve as a hoplite (a foot-solider in Ancient Greece), it does not cover what life was like for Spartan girls.*

Unit Notes

Authors' note about this week's reading:

This week's reading covers the development of Greece, with a special focus on the city-state of Sparta. One aspect of Spartan society that parents should be forewarned about is the practice of infant abandonment. If a baby was born in Sparta with a disability, the baby would be left alone to die in the wild. The Spartans' main goal was the greatness of Sparta, and they believed there was no place in their society for children with disabilities. This idea may be quite upsetting to students with disabilities, or students who have friends, relatives, or neighbors with disabilities. So, basically, it may be upsetting to pretty much everyone. This is a good opportunity to discuss how disabilities have been viewed throughout history and how far people with disabilities have come in their fight for equal rights . . . and how far there still is to go.

UNIT 15

CLASSICAL GREECE

This Week's Quest

Learn about ancient Greece's classical time, when the city-state of Athens came up with a brand-new way to govern.

Resources & Materials

History Quest: Early Times (HQ)

Usborne Encyclopedia of World History with Internet Links (UEWH)

History Travel Log page and The Citizen illustration (Appendix C)

Enrichment Reading

The Librarian who Measured the Earth by Kathryn Lasky

Everyday Life in Ancient Greece by Anne Pearson

Supplies Needed for Day 3

- Paper plates
- Markers/paint/dot-art supplies
- Scissors
- Craft sticks
- Tape
- Optional: other items to decorate your mask

Unit Schedule

Day 1 Discover	Day 2 Explore	Day 3 Create	Day 4 Demonstrate	Day 5 Enrich
UEWH pages 158–159	History Hop! The Citizen	Make Greek Comedy and Tragedy Masks	Review Terms & Concepts	Explore Pandia Web Links
HQ Chapter 15 Classical Greece	Google Earth		Complete one or more review options	Read from Enrichment Reading list
	History Travel Log			

Terms & Concepts

The Big Ideas

❋ The Athenians are famous for their interesting ideas and their beautiful buildings and art.

❋ Athens was the first place to have a democracy, which is a government where the citizens make decisions. The only people who could vote in Athens were adult men who were born in Athens.

❋ The place where Athenians gathered to buy and sell things and talk about government decisions was called the Agora.

The Details

❋ A person could be kicked out of ancient Athens for ten years if enough citizens voted for this to happen. This is called *ostracism*.

❋ Athens and Sparta fought a war called the Peloponnesian War because Sparta worried that Athens was getting too strong. Sparta won that war.

❋ The Peloponnesian War and other battles between the city-states weakened the ancient Greeks. This made it easier for the city-states to be conquered once the Macedonians to the north got stronger.

Lessons

Day 1. Discover

- ☐ **Read pages 158–159 in UEWH.** If desired, navigate to some of the websites recommended in the book.
- ☐ **Read Chapter 15: Classical Greece in HQ pages 249–259**

Day 2. Explore

- ☐ **Read History Hop! The Citizen in HQ pages 260–270**
- ☐ **Google Earth.** Search for "Parthenon" to check out this archaeological site.
- ☐ **History Travel Log.** Complete the travel log page for this unit and place it in your history notebook.

Day 3. Create

- ☐ **Craft: Make Greek Comedy and Tragedy Masks**

Supplies:

- 2 paper plates (or use poster board)
- Scissors
- Markers, painting supplies, or dot-art daubers to color the masks
- 2 craft sticks
- Tape
- Optional: other items to decorate the masks, such as yarn, chenille sticks to add hair, washi tape, markers, etc.

The ancient Greeks participated in open-air theatre, and they needed a way for people even in the worst seats to get a sense of what the actors were portraying. They wore masks with exaggerated facial expressions so that even those who were quite far from the stage could understand what was going on in the story. While most actors nowadays don't wear masks like these on stage anymore, the comedy and tragedy masks have become a symbol of theatre.

Directions:

Draw (or paint) exaggerated eyes, nose, and mouths on the two paper plates. To represent the extremes of human emotion, one mask should have a giant grin, and the other should have a piteous frown. Cut out facial features (it might help if you get each cut started for the child) and color/decorate the mask however you like. Remember that one of the masks should look profoundly happy, and the other should look horribly sad. Attach your masks to the craft sticks with tape, so your child is able to hold a mask up to their face.

Day 4. Demonstrate

- ☐ **Read through the Terms & Concepts.** Optional: Copy some or all of the Terms & Concepts into your history notebook.
- ☐ **Complete one or more of the following** in order to strengthen your child's knowledge of the material and to provide an opportunity for you to evaluate their understanding:

Option #1 Short Answers

Answer the following questions verbally or write them in your history notebook:

Q: What kind of government did Athens invent?
A: *Athens invented democracy.*

Q: Which two Greek city-states fought each other in the Peloponnesian War, and who won?
A: *Athens and Sparta fought. Sparta won.*

Q: Now that you know a little about Athens and Sparta, which one would you want to live in if you had to choose, and why?
A: *Answers may vary. Possible responses include: I would pick Athens because I don't want to be a soldier or, I would pick Sparta because it was a better place to be a girl.*

Option #2 Narration

Answer the following verbally or in writing:

- List three important things you learned about the Classical Greek civilization.

Option #3 Copywork/Dictation

Copy or write from dictation one of the following into your history notebook:

Democracy was invented in Athens. It also had beautiful buildings and art.

Athens was famous for its beautiful buildings and art. The Athenians also invented democracy, which means "rule by the people."

Day 5. Enrich

☐ **Visit www.pandiapress.com/weblinks.** There you will find a description of some recommended websites related to this unit.

☐ **Read one or more from the Enrichment Reading list**

The Librarian who Measured the Earth by Kathryn Lasky. A simply delightful book about a not-so-well-known ancient Greek, Eratosthenes. Technically, this book doesn't fit into this unit because Eratosthenes lived later, but he is such a good representation of the best that Classical Greece had to offer that his inclusion is warranted. Lasky's text and Kevin Hawkes's illustrations set this book well above the average.

Everyday Life in Ancient Greece by Anne Pearson. This book comes from a series called *Clues to the Past*, which also includes titles on Egypt, Rome, and the Vikings. It covers aspects of daily life such as eating, clothing, hairstyles, sports, and theater. A couple of pages are dedicated to explaining how separate men and women were, even within the home, which could lead to some interesting discussions.

Unit Notes

UNIT 16

MACEDONIAN EMPIRE

This Week's Quest

Learn about an empire that started as a neighbor to the Greeks and ended up being the largest empire of its time.

Resources & Materials

History Quest: Early Times (HQ)

Usborne Encyclopedia of World History with Internet Links (UEWH)

Map 6 (Appendix C)

History Travel Log page and The General illustration (Appendix C)

Supplies Needed for Day 3

- Pictures of animals
- Poster board/construction paper
- Markers
- Glue

Enrichment Reading

Alexander the Great by Demi

Unit Schedule

Day 1 Discover	Day 2 Explore	Day 3 Create	Day 4 Demonstrate	Day 5 Enrich
UEWH pages 160–161	History Hop! The General	Classify Like Aristotle	Review Terms & Concepts	Explore Pandia Web Links
HQ Chapter 16 Macedonian Empire	History Travel Log		Complete one or more review options	Read from Enrichment Reading list
Map 6				

Terms & Concepts

The Big Ideas

- King Philip started the Macedonian empire. Later, in 338 BCE, he conquered the Greeks and became their leader, too.
- Philip's son, Alexander the Great, became the new leader of the Macedonian empire at age 20 when his father was killed. He grew his empire to include Macedonia, Greece, Egypt, Persia, and more lands. It was the largest empire ever at the time.

The Details

- As a boy, Alexander was tutored by the famous Greek philosopher, Aristotle. He also tamed a wild horse when grown men couldn't, and he acted as a leader in the army when he was a teenager.
- A famous story about Alexander involves the Gordian knot. This was a big knot of rope that no one could figure out how to undo. People said that whoever could undo the knot would become the master of the world. Instead of trying to untie the knot with his fingers, clever Alexander just cut through it with his sword.
- Alexander died on his way home from conquering many lands in 323 BCE. He was only 32 years old. After he died, his empire was divided up.

Lessons

Day 1. Discover

- ☐ **Read pages 160-161 in UEWH.** If desired, navigate to some of the websites recommended in the book.
- ☐ **Read Chapter 16: Macedonian Empire in HQ pages 271–281**
  ** Refer to the end of this unit for an authors' note about the reading this week.*
- ☐ **Complete Map 6.** Referring to the map in HQ on page 279 and UEWH on page 160:
  1. Label these bodies of water:
     Arabian Sea
     Persian Gulf
     Nile River
     Red Sea
     Caspian Sea
     Black Sea
     Mediterranean Sea
  2. Label these civilizations/areas:
     MACEDONIA
     GREECE
     EGYPT
     PERSIA
     INDIA
     MESOPOTAMIA
  3. Label these cities:
     •Babylon
     •Gordium
     •Guagamela
  4. Shade the empire of Alexander the Great.

Day 2. Explore

☐ **Read History Hop! The General in HQ pages 282–289**

☐ **History Travel Log.** Complete the travel log page for this unit and place it in your history notebook.

Day 3. Create

☐ **Classify Like Aristotle**

Supplies:

- Pictures of six or more different animals—preferably pictures you can cut out or print out
- Poster board or large piece of construction paper
- Markers
- Glue

Alexander the Great's tutor, Aristotle, was not only a great philosopher, but also a great scientist. He was one of the first people to try to understand the natural world in a systematic way—he created the first classification system that we know about. He divided animals into land, water, and air groups, based on where they lived. Plants were divided into small, medium, and large by size.

Directions:

Give your child an opportunity to classify different animals. First, talk through Aristotle's division of animals into land, water, and air categories. Ask for examples for each. Then ask if there are any animals that don't fit easily into any of those categories. (A frog is a good example of this. You can also talk about flightless birds and whether a bee should be in the same category as an eagle.)

Brainstorm with your child all the different ways you can divide up the animals. You can choose by size, color, where the animals live, how many legs they have, etc. You can also encourage your child to get a little unscientific by classifying animals based on other more subjective traits, like how smelly, cuddly, or cute they are! Depending on the age of your child, decide whether you will have two, three, or four categories. List the title of the project and the names of the various categories on the poster board. Paste the pictures of the different animals within their proper categories.

Day 4. Demonstrate

☐ **Read through the Terms & Concepts.** Optional: Copy some or all of the Terms & Concepts into your history notebook.

☐ **Complete one or more of the following** in order to strengthen your child's knowledge of the material and to provide an opportunity for you to evaluate their understanding:

Option #1 Short Answers

Answer the following questions verbally or write them in your history notebook:

Q: How do the legends say Alexander the Great solved the problem of the Gordian knot?

A: Instead of untying it, he just cut through it with a sword.

Q: Can you name some of the places that Philip and Alexander took over when they were building the Macedonian Empire?

A: They took over Greece, Egypt, Persia, and other lands.

Q: What happened to Alexander's empire after he died at a very young age?

A: The empire was split.

Option #2 Narration

Answer the following verbally or in writing:

- List three important things you learned about the Macedonian Empire.

Option #3 Copywork

Copy or write from dictation one of the following into your history notebook:

> Alexander the Great ruled the Macedonians and conquered lots of other lands.

The Macedonians lived near Greece. Their king, Philip, started the Macedonian Empire when he took over Greece. Philip's son, Alexander the Great, made an even bigger empire when he conquered Persia, Egypt, and other lands.

Day 5. Enrich

- ☐ **Visit www.pandiapress.com/weblinks.** There you will find a description of some recommended websites related to this unit.
- ☐ **Read from the Enrichment Reading list**

  Alexander the Great by Demi. Simple, but not childish, text and wonderful illustrations from the noted children's author.

Unit Notes

Authors' note about this week's reading:

Whether the ancient Macedonians (and Alexander the Great) were Greek or not Greek is an important issue for a number of people. This curriculum does not make the degree of Alexander's "Greekness" a priority. However, Macedonians are talked about as a distinct group, not simply as northern Greeks.

Most of the information we have about Philip and Alexander came from writers who lived a few generations later. Thus, whether Demosthenes actually practiced with pebbles in his mouth, whether Alexander tamed Bucephalus in the manner reported, whether Alexander was bossed around by Diogenes, or whether the legendary undoing of the Gordian knot ever happened—we can't know for certain.

UNIT 17

INDIA: PART ONE

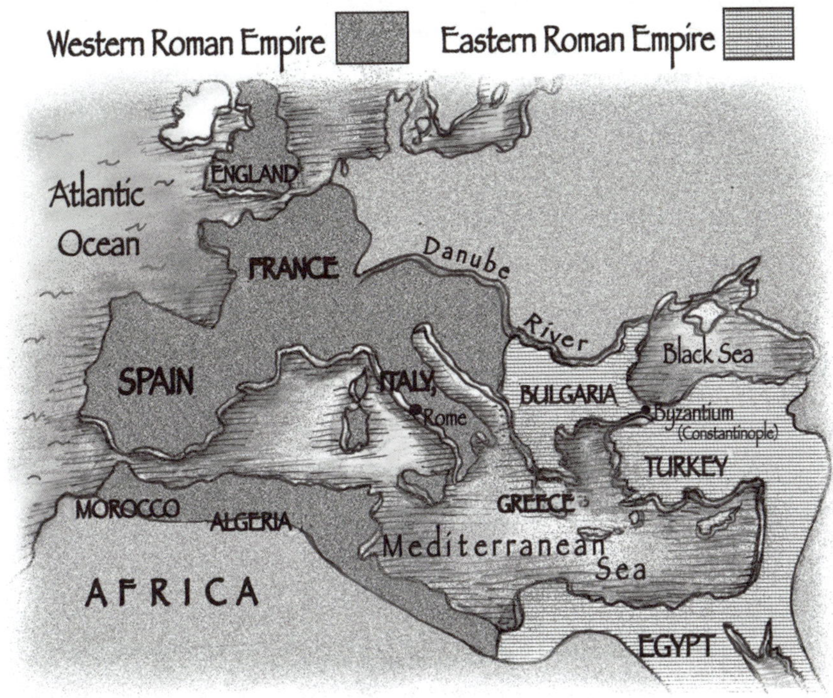

This Week's Quest

Learn about an ancient civilization that liked to keep things neat and organized. In fact, they were so neat that they even had indoor plumbing!

Resources & Materials

History Quest: Early Times (HQ)

Usborne Encyclopedia of World History with Internet Links (UEWH)

Map 7 (Appendix C)

History Travel Log page and The City Planner illustration (Appendix C)

Supplies Needed for Day 3

Option 1

- Paper
- Markers

Option 2

- Clay/modeling dough
- Carving tool

Enrichment Reading

Building History: Indus Valley City by Gillian Clements

The Indus Valley by Jane Shuter

Unit Schedule

Day 1 Discover	Day 2 Explore	Day 3 Create	Day 4 Demonstrate	Day 5 Enrich
UEWH pages 118–119	History Hop! The City Planner	Make an Indus Valley Seal with a Secret Language	Review Terms & Concepts	Explore Pandia Web Links
HQ Chapter 17 India: Part One	Google Earth		Complete one or more review options	Read from Enrichment Reading list
Map 7	History Travel Log			

Terms & Concepts

The Big Ideas

❋ Historians used to think that ancient Indian civilization began when a group of outsiders called the Aryans moved in, but actually, it began with the Harappan (also called Indus Valley) civilization around 3300 BCE.

❋ Harappan civilization was famous for its neatly designed cities, clean water, and innovative indoor plumbing. The most famous city in the Harappan Civilization was Mohenjo-daro.

❋ The Aryans were in charge of India from about 1500 BCE to about 500 BCE. They are known for bringing the Hindu religion to India.

The Details

❋ The Aryans were more concerned with fighting each other than just about anything else. They liked to write and paint about fighting.

❋ The Aryans introduced the caste system into ancient India as part of the Hindu religion. In the caste system, people are born into one of four main social groups and could never leave those groups.

❋ Hindus believe in reincarnation, karma, and nirvana. Reincarnation is a belief that a person keeps being reborn over and over again after dying, sometimes as other people, sometimes as animals. Karma is the belief that people will always be rewarded or punished for what they do. Nirvana is a state of perfect peace that a person achieves once they are worthy.

Lessons

Day 1. Discover

- ☐ **Read pages 118–119 in UEWH.** If desired, navigate to some of the websites recommended in the book.
- ☐ **Read Chapter 17: India: Part One in HQ pages 291–300**
  ** Refer to the end of this unit for an authors' note about the reading this week.*
- ☐ **Complete Map 7.** Referring to the map in HQ on page 291 add the following labels:
  1. Label these bodies of water:
     Arabian Sea
     Indian Ocean
     Bay of Bengal
     Indus River
     Ganges River
  2. Label these cities:
     •Mohenjo-daro
     •Harappa
  3. Label the following:
     INDIA
     PAKISTAN
     HIMALAYAS
  4. Draw triangles to indicate the Himalayas.

Day 2. Explore

- ☐ **Read History Hop! The City Planner in HQ pages 301–310**
- ☐ **Google Earth.** Search for "Harappa" and click on the image to see this dig site.
- ☐ **History Travel Log.** Complete the travel log page for this unit and place it in your history notebook.

Day 3. Create

☐ **Craft: Make an Indus Valley Seal with a Secret Language**

Supplies:

- Paper and a marker (if drawing seal)
- Clay/modeling dough and a carving tool (if carving seal)

Directions:

Think of a simple secret message to put on the seal—a short word or phrase on the top and on the bottom. It could include your name, the name of your favorite sports team, pet, etc. Then, come up with your own secret symbol to correspond with each English letter. Think of a design for the seal. Put your secret message across the top and/or the bottom, with an animal of your choice in the middle.

The most authentic way to to make the seal is to use clay, such as Sculpey, that is baked to harden. But using materials like Crayola Model Magic or even paper and markers is also perfectly acceptable.

c. 2200 BCE Indus Valley seal featuring a unicorn

Indus Valley seal craft featuring a red panda

Day 4. Demonstrate

☐ **Read through the Terms & Concepts.** Optional: Copy some or all of the Terms & Concepts into your history notebook.

☐ **Complete one or more of the following** in order to strengthen your child's knowledge of the material and to provide an opportunity for you to evaluate their understanding:

Option #1 Short Answers

Answer the following questions verbally or write them in your history notebook:

Q: What was the Harappan civilization famous for?

A: *Harappan civilization had orderly cities and clean water. They even had toilets.*

Q: What religion did the Aryans bring to India?

A: *They brought Hinduism to India.*

Q: What is a caste system?

A: *The caste system is where people are born into different levels in society, and they have to stay in the same level throughout their lives.*

Option #2 Narration

Answer the following verbally or in writing:

- List three important things you learned about ancient Indian civilization.

Option #3 Copywork

Copy or write from dictation one of the following into your history notebook:

The Indus Valley civilization had clean water, straight roads, and even toilets!

Ancient India had a really old civilization called the Indus Valley civilization. The people of that civilization made orderly cities where they had plenty of water, straight roads, and even toilets. Later, a group called the Aryans came to India. The Aryans liked to fight and they brought Hinduism and the caste system.

Day 5. Enrich

☐ **Visit www.pandiapress.com/weblinks.** There you will find a description of some recommended websites related to this unit.

☐ **Read from the Enrichment Reading list**

Building History: Indus Valley City by Gillian Clements. Very well-designed and well-written overview of Indus Valley civilization. If you choose just one book to support the learning of this material, this is the one to choose.

The Indus Valley by Jane Shuter. This book from the *History Opens Windows* series covers cities, family and home life, beliefs, and other aspects of life in the ancient Indus Valley. It includes some excellent photos of Indus Valley plumbing and drainage systems.

Unit Notes

Authors' note about this week's reading:

History Quest*'s coverage of ancient Indian civilization includes regions now in countries other than modern-day India, including Pakistan and Bangladesh. Even referring to this material as "Ancient Indian History" is controversial in some quarters because the term only names India.*

Some units introduce students to world religions (like Hinduism, Jainism, and Buddhism) that are far more complicated than History Quest *can cover for its intended age group. These religions each have their variants as well. By necessity, we present very simplified explanations of these religions. Please keep this in mind, particularly if your family follows one of these faiths. Similarly,* History Quest*'s explanation of how the caste system works is also quite simplified due to space constraints and the intended age of the reader. In addition, it should be noted that the modern country of India has been working to counteract the oppressive aspects of the traditional social system.*

UNIT 18

INDIA: PART TWO

This Week's Quest

Learn about the founder of the Mauryan empire and his grandson—a man who made major changes in his lifestyle and beliefs in order to become "Great."

Resources & Materials

History Quest: Early Times (HQ)

Usborne Encyclopedia of World History with Internet Links (UEWH)

History Travel Log page and The Converted illustration (Appendix C)

Enrichment Reading

The Elephant's Friend and Other Tales from Ancient India by Marcia Williams

Ganesha's Sweet Tooth by Sanjay Patel and Emily Haynes

Supplies Needed for Day 3

- Red kidney beans
- Cooking oil
- Cumin seeds
- Onions
- Fresh ginger
- Fresh garlic
- Tomatoes
- Green chilies (fresh or canned)
- Spice powders: coriander, cumin, garam masala, turmeric
- Salt
- Water
- Optional: asafetida, cilantro, rice or naan bread

Unit Schedule

Day 1 Discover	Day 2 Explore	Day 3 Create	Day 4 Demonstrate	Day 5 Enrich
UEWH pages 174–175	History Hop! The Converted	Make a Dish Fit for Ashoka	Review Terms & Concepts	Explore Pandia Web Links
HQ Chapter 18 India: Part Two	History Travel Log		Complete one or more review options	Read from Enrichment Reading list

Terms & Concepts

The Big Ideas

- The Mauryan Empire began when Chandragupta Maurya conquered many separate kingdoms. Chandragupta was a good leader who helped his empire become richer and safer.
- Ashoka was Chandragupta's grandson who made the Mauryan Empire even bigger and more powerful. After conquering the kingdom of Kalinga in a very bloody battle, Ashoka had a change of heart and became a peaceful Buddhist. He became known as Ashoka the Great because he tried to make life better for his people.

The Details

- Jainism is another religion that started in ancient India and still exists today. Jains believe that everything is alive and in order to reach nirvana you need to stop, or at least lessen, doing any violence to anything.
- The religion of Buddhism began in ancient India 2,500 years ago. Buddhists believe that people should always do good so they can escape being reincarnated again and again and reach nirvana.

Lessons

Day 1. Discover

- ☐ **Read pages 174–175 in UEWH.** If desired, navigate to some of the websites recommended in the book.
- ☐ **Read Chapter 18: India: Part Two in HQ pages 311–318**
  ** Refer to the end of this unit for an authors' note about the reading this week.*

Day 2. Explore

- ☐ **Read History Hop! The Converted in HQ pages 319–328**
- ☐ **History Travel Log.** Complete the travel log page for this unit and place it in your history notebook.

Day 3. Create

- ☐ **Cooking: Make a Dish Fit for Ashoka**

Supplies:

- 1 can red kidney beans
- 2 tablespoons cooking oil
- 1 teaspoon cumin seeds
- 2 medium onions, chopped
- 2 pieces ginger (about 1 inch each), chopped
- 5-6 cloves of garlic, minced
- 2 large tomatoes, diced into 1-inch cubes
- 2 fresh green chilies (remove seeds), chopped, OR ½ can green chilies, chopped
- 2 teaspoons coriander powder
- 1 teaspoon cumin
- 1 teaspoon garam masala (available in the spice aisle)
- ¼ teaspoon turmeric
- Salt to taste
- 3 cups water
- Optional: pinch of asafetida
- Optional: chopped cilantro (fresh coriander)
- Optional: rice or naan for serving

Ashoka would have loved this North Indian vegetarian dish, although not all of the ingredients you are using here would have been available to him. Parents will need to be much more hands-on with this cooking activity. All instructions are directed toward an adult, but parents will know which steps can be handled by their children. Note: This recipe also works well in an electric pressure cooker on the "sauté" setting.

Directions:

Rinse the kidney beans in a colander. Heat the oil in a deep pan over medium high heat. Add the cumin seeds and stir while they sizzle. When the sizzling stops, add the onions and continue to fry until the onions are soft, about another five minutes. No need to brown them. Next, add the ginger and garlic and stir another 1-2 minutes. Make sure they don't stick to the bottom and burn. Then add the tomatoes, green chilies, ground coriander, ground cumin, garam masala, and turmeric. Fry, stirring, for about 3 more minutes. Next, add the kidney beans, salt, water, and/or the optional asafetida and cilantro. Cook for another 10 minutes. Serve with rice or naan bread.

Day 4. Demonstrate

- ☐ **Read through the Terms & Concepts.** Optional: Copy some or all of the Terms & Concepts into your history notebook.
- ☐ **Complete one or more of the following** in order to strengthen your child's knowledge of the material and to provide an opportunity for you to evaluate their understanding:

Option #1 Short Answers

Answer the following questions verbally or write them in your history notebook:

Q: What is the name of the ruling dynasty that Chandragupta started?

A: He started the Mauryan Dynasty.

Q: What kind of ruler was Ashoka when he started, and how did he change?

A: Ashoka wanted to conquer people when he started, but he changed his mind and became peaceful, and tried to protect people and animals.

Q: Besides Hinduism, which other two religions started in ancient India?

A: Jainism and Buddhism both started in ancient India.

Option #2 Narration

Answer the following verbally or in writing:

- List three important things you learned about ancient Indian civilization.

Option #3 Copywork/Dictation

Copy or write from dictation one of the following into your history notebook:

Ashoka was mean at first, but then he changed and tried to make life better for people and animals.

Chandragupta Maurya began the Mauryan Empire in India by taking over hundreds of other kingdoms. His grandson, Ashoka the Great, made the Mauryan Empire even bigger and stronger. At first, Ashoka was very mean, but later, he changed his ways and tried to make life better for everyone.

Day 5. Enrich

- ☐ **Visit www.pandiapress.com/weblinks.** There you will find a description of some recommended websites related to this unit.
- ☐ **Read one or more from the Enrichment Reading list**

  The Elephant's Friend and Other Tales from Ancient India by Marcia Williams. Beloved children's writer cleverly recasts these Indian tales in both her visuals and her writing.

  Ganesha's Sweet Tooth by Sanjay Patel and Emily Haynes. Traditional tale illustrated in a very non-traditional but lovely way.

Unit Notes

Authors' note about this week's reading:

Similar to the previous unit, this unit introduces students to Buddhism and Jainism. By necessity, the explanations of both of these religions have been simplified.

History Quest *presents Ashoka the way legend has always presented him—as a man who was unbelievably ruthless in his early years, only to repent thoroughly after his one and only battle, devoting the rest of his life to living out his Buddhist beliefs. Some historians believe that these legends may have overestimated both Ashoka's earlier cruelty and his later transformation in order to promote Buddhism. Other historians claim that Ashoka's "repentance" was motivated by political expediency. However, there is plenty of evidence supporting the legends in this case and we really don't have any evidence that significantly undermines their veracity.*

HYGGE HISTORY #3

THE *RAMAYANA*

This Week's Quest

- Read and enjoy classic Indian literature.

Resources

Ramayana: Divine Loophole by Sanjay Patel (ISBN 978-0811871075)

Hygge History

This week, you and your child will be visiting ancient India to watch an expert archer with electric blue skin take on a nasty demon with ten heads in the *Ramayana* [RHA-mah-YAH-nah]. The *Ramayana* is one of ancient India's two most famous epics; the other is the *Mahabharata*. The *Ramayana* tells the story of Rama, a human avatar of the Hindu god Vishnu, as he endures a fourteen-year exile from his kingdom with his wife Sita and loyal brother Lakshman. When the evil demon Ravana kidnaps Sita, Rama and his many allies must spring into action to save her.

Besides just being a generally suspenseful and exciting story, the *Ramayana*, like the *Iliad*, explores themes of loyalty, devotion, honor, and creative problem-solving. And, like our pick for a children's version of the *Iliad*, we are once again looking to an illustrator who is better known for his work on the silver screen. *Ramayana: Divine Loophole* is retold and illustrated by Sanjay Patel, who also happens to be an animator at Pixar. If you are a fan of Pixar animation, you will certainly notice a familiar style in the book's stunning illustrations.

Before you read, here are a few things to know. First, the original text of the *Ramayana* is about 24,000 verses long! That means that the children's version is not going to contain every last detail from the original. Also, Patel's version is written with a twenty-first-century audience in mind. He uses modern phrases and a conversational style, quite different from the poetic writing style we saw in McCaughrean's version of *Gilgamesh* or Sutcliff's version of the *Iliad*. Patel's rendition is excellently suited to an audience that has never heard the story before. Thanks to his conversational style and illustrations that move the story along, parents should not find themselves constantly stopping to explain what's going on.

When you receive your copy of the book, you might notice it is quite lengthy. Not to worry—the story of the *Ramayana* is only about the first two-thirds of the pages. The rest of the book is dedicated to (very helpful) profiles of gods, warriors, animal characters, and demons from Hindu mythology. Also, even within the story section of the book, the illustrations take up most of the page. The story is told in three acts, and you should be able to manage about one act per day over three days' time.

Enjoy this delightful and visually stunning trip into the literature of ancient India!

Hygge History Notes

UNIT 19

ROMAN REPUBLIC

This Week's Quest

Learn how Rome got its start and grew into a powerful republic.

Resources & Materials

History Quest: Early Times (HQ)

Usborne Encyclopedia of World History with Internet Links (UEWH)

Map 8 (Appendix C)

History Travel Log page and The Veteran illustration (Appendix C)

Enrichment Reading

DK Eyewitness Books: Ancient Rome by Simon James

Supplies Needed for Day 3

- Plastic spoon
- Craft sticks
- Wine cork or empty thread spool
- Rubber bands
- Small, light objects to launch (e.g. mini marshmallows)

Unit Schedule

Day 1 Discover	Day 2 Explore	Day 3 Create	Day 4 Demonstrate	Day 5 Enrich
UEWH pages 184–185	History Hop! The Veteran	Make a Roman Catapult	Review Terms & Concepts	Explore Pandia Web Links
HQ Chapter 19 Roman Republic	History Travel Log		Complete one or more review options	Read from Enrichment Reading list
Map 8				

Terms & Concepts

The Big Ideas

❋ Rome is in present-day Italy. It was built near the Tiber River.

❋ At first, Rome was ruled by kings. But after about 250 years, they kicked out their last king and decided they would never have a king again. They turned their government into a republic—a government where citizens can vote on who the rulers should be.

❋ The most important wars fought during the time of the Roman Republic were called the Punic Wars, fought against the powerful city of Carthage. There were three Punic Wars.

❋ Hannibal was a great Carthaginian general who almost defeated Rome for good. He surprised the Romans by crossing the Alps with a big army and war elephants.

The Details

❋ Roman legend says that the city was founded by two royal brothers who were left for dead but taken care of by a wolf mother. The brothers were called Romulus and Remus. Romulus killed his brother and named the city Rome after himself.

❋ Roman society was divided into patricians and plebeians. Patricians were more powerful.

❋ As Rome became richer and more powerful, some people within the Roman Empire began to have more and more problems. Veterans and poor people had a hard time living in the later Roman Republic, partly because Romans were using more and more slaves to do work rather than hiring workers and paying them.

Lessons

Day 1. Discover

- ☐ **Read pages 184–185 in UEWH.** If desired, navigate to some of the websites recommended in the book.
- ☐ **Read Chapter 19: Roman Republic in HQ pages 329–341**
- ☐ **Complete Map 8.** Referring to the map in HQ on page 330 and UEWH on page 184:

1. Label these bodies of water:

   Tiber River

   Rubicon River

   Mediterranean Sea

2. Label these countries/regions:

   SICILY

   CRETE

   SPAIN

   ITALY

   GREECE

   GAUL

3. Label these cities:

   •Carthage

   •Rome

4. Draw triangles to indicate the Alps.

Day 2. Explore

- ☐ **Read History Hop! The Veteran in HQ pages 342–352**
- ☐ **History Travel Log.** Complete the travel log page for this unit and place it in your history notebook.

Day 3. Create

☐ **Craft: Make a Roman Catapult**

Supplies:

- Plastic spoon
- 2 craft sticks (or more, in case your first attempt causes breakage)
- Wine cork or empty thread spool (or other small cylindrical item)
- 2 rubber bands
- Light, small objects to launch (mini marshmallows, oyster crackers, etc.)

The Romans were not the first people to use a catapult in their battles. But it was one of their favorite weapons when they came upon walled cities. This simple craft helps your child understand some of the physics behind the sort of catapult the Romans would have used.

Directions:

Using one rubber band, attach the plastic spoon to the end of one of the sticks. Align it so that the "bowl" part of the spoon hangs just beyond the stick. Line the second craft stick under the first one and rubber band them together at the other end. Carefully separating the two sticks at the spoon end, push the cork between them until the cork rests somewhere in the middle. Line up your catapult and place your mini marshmallow/oyster cracker in the spoon. Push the spoon down and release.

You can come up with variations on the catapult to test which designs work the best. Try pushing the cork closer to the spoon to see how that affects the distance of the projectile. Try using projectiles of different weights. You can also rubber band slightly overlapped craft sticks together to make longer arms.

For families who wish to learn more, there are many videos related to Roman catapults online. Some are produced by historical or museum groups. Others are designed to show you how to create a more sophisticated Roman catapult of your own. Enter "Roman catapult craft" in a Google search to see the many variations on this idea.

Day 4. Demonstrate

☐ **Read through the Terms & Concepts.** Optional: Copy some or all of the Terms & Concepts into your history notebook.

☐ **Complete one or more of the following** in order to strengthen your child's knowledge of the material and to provide an opportunity for you to evaluate their understanding:

Option #1 Short Answers

Answer the following questions verbally or write them in your history notebook:

Q: In which modern-day country is the city of Rome?

A: *Rome is located in Italy.*

Q: After the Romans decided they didn't want to be ruled by kings, what kind of government did they have?

A: *They had a republic, where citizens get to vote on who their rulers should be.*

Q: Roman society was separated into patricians and plebeians. Which group had more power?

A: *The patricians had more power.*

Option #2 Narration

Answer the following verbally or in writing:

- List three important things you learned about the Roman Republic.

Option #3 Copywork

Copy or write from dictation one of the following into your history notebook:

> Rome was first ruled by kings. Then it became a republic.

> The Roman Republic began in the city of Rome in 509 BCE. It became a mighty empire. Rome fought against Carthage in the Punic Wars. Romans were not supposed to care very much about money or power. But some Romans like Julius Caesar wanted to become more and more powerful.

Day 5. Enrich

- ☐ **Visit www.pandiapress.com/weblinks.** There you will find a description of some recommended websites related to this unit.
- ☐ **Read from the Enrichment Reading list**

  DK Eyewitness Books: Ancient Rome by Simon James. Another in DK's *Eyewitness* series, full of the expected photographs and details. Note that some of the material applies to later Roman history, so this would be a good book to reference across the three units devoted to Rome.

Unit Notes

UNIT 20

ROMAN EMPIRE

This Week's Quest

Learn how Rome changed from a republic into an empire and completed many amazing building projects.

Resources & Materials

History Quest: Early Times (HQ)

Usborne Encyclopedia of World History with Internet Links (UEWH)

History Travel Log page and The Engineer illustration (Appendix C)

Enrichment Reading

Cleopatra by Diane Stanley

Pompeii…Buried Alive! by Edith Kunhardt

City: A Story of Roman Planning and Construction by David Macauley

Supplies Needed for Day 3

- Pencil
- Ruler
- Construction paper
- Scissors
- Poster board/card stock
- Glue

Unit Schedule

Day 1 Discover	Day 2 Explore	Day 3 Create	Day 4 Demonstrate	Day 5 Enrich
UEWH pages 182-183, 186–191	History Hop! The Engineer	Make a Roman Mosaic	Review Terms & Concepts	Explore Pandia Web Links
HQ Chapter 20 Roman Empire	Google Earth		Complete one or more review options	Read from Enrichment Reading list
	History Travel Log			

Terms & Concepts

The Big Ideas

- Julius Caesar was a leader at the end of the Roman Republic who became more and more powerful. Senators assassinated him because they were worried he had too much power.
- Julius Caesar's adopted son, Octavian, became the first emperor of the Roman Empire. He made many changes to try to help the people of Rome.
- Rome was famous for its building projects, including aqueducts, arches, vaults, buildings such as the Colosseum and Pantheon, and the best roads ever built during ancient times.

The Details

- The Pax Romana is the name given for the first 200 years of the Roman Empire. Pax Romana means "peace of Rome."
- Mount Vesuvius was a volcano that erupted in 79 CE. The ash, rocks, and hot gas that came out of the volcano killed thousands of people.

Lessons

Day 1. Discover

- ☐ **Read pages 182–183 and 186–191 in UEWH.** If desired, navigate to some of the websites recommended in the book.
- ☐ **Read Chapter 20: Roman Empire in HQ pages 353–362**
  ** Refer to the end of this unit for an authors' note about the reading this week.*

Day 2. Explore

- ☐ **Read History Hop! The Engineer in HQ pages 363–372**
- ☐ **Google Earth.** Search for "Pantheon" and you can get a close-up look. You can even see the oculus!
- ☐ **History Travel Log.** Complete the travel log page for this unit and place it in your history notebook.

Day 3. Create

- ☐ **Craft: Make a Roman Mosaic**

Supplies:

- Pencil
- Ruler
- Various colors of construction paper
- Scissors
- Poster board or card stock
- Glue

One of the Romans' favorite ways of decorating their floors and walls was by creating mosaics. You can approximate a Roman mosaic using construction paper. It might be a good idea to look for images online for Roman mosaics. You can base your design on a traditional Roman idea or come up with one of your own.

Directions:

Using the ruler and pencil, mark ½-inch squares on one of the sheets of construction paper. Stack two or three sheets under and cut through them to create your "tiles." Repeat this process until you have as many tiles as you need.

Sketch out a simple scene, face, or geometric design on the poster board. Don't include too many details. Plan ahead which colors will fill in which parts of your mosaic.

Put a little glue on the back of a square and paste it to the poster board. Complete the picture with the other squares, making sure to leave a small gap between the squares.

Day 4. Demonstrate

- ☐ **Read through the Terms & Concepts.** Optional: Copy some or all of the Terms & Concepts into your history notebook.
- ☐ **Complete one or more of the following** in order to strengthen your child's knowledge of the material and to provide an opportunity for you to evaluate their understanding:

Option #1 Short Answers

Answer the following questions verbally or write them in your history notebook:

Q: What happened to Julius Caesar when the senators thought he was getting too powerful?
A: *They assassinated him.*

Q: Who became the emperor once Caesar died?
A: *Octavian (or Caesar Augustus) became the first emperor.*

Q: What happened to the Roman city of Pompeii?
A: *It was buried under ash after a volcano called Mt. Vesuvius erupted.*

Option #2 Narration

Answer the following verbally or in writing:

- List three important things you learned about the Roman Empire.

Option #3 Copywork/Dictation

Copy or write from dictation one of the following into your history notebook:

> During the Roman Empire, Romans built roads, aqueducts, and beautiful buildings.

> The Roman Empire began when Caesar Augustus became emperor in 27 BCE. The time after Augustus began ruling was called the Pax Romana. During this time, Rome built many roads, aqueducts, and beautiful buildings

Day 5. Enrich

☐ **Visit www.pandiapress.com/weblinks.** There you will find a description of some recommended websites related to this unit.

☐ **Read one or more from the Enrichment Reading list**

Cleopatra by Diane Stanley. Stanley writes enthralling biographies, all accompanied by excellent illustrations. *Cleopatra* is no exception, and reading it will allow the student to learn more about the Roman conquest of Egypt and the story of Egypt's final pharaoh. Highly recommended.

Pompeii…Buried Alive! by Edith Kunhardt. Telling the complicated and spine-chilling story of the eruption of Mount Vesuvius and the destruction of a thriving Roman city for a young audience would be challenging under any circumstances, but Kunhardt manages to go one step further, turning this into a "Step into Reading" format (Level 4). Text and illustrations keep children in mind, avoiding the more disturbing details.

City: A Story of Roman Planning and Construction by David Macauley. Macauley is an author who has shared his brilliant teaching style with learning families all over the world. *City* focuses on the building of a Roman city, turning complicated technical matters into an accessible story. *City* is not for the youngest students, but older students should be given the chance to give this remarkable book a *try. A PBS documentary based on this book, called* Roman City, *is also available. Like the book, it too is recommended. But parents should consider introducing the book before the documentary, especially to older students.*

Unit Notes

Authors' note about this week's reading:

Throughout human history, people have done terrible things to each other. Some Roman emperors were particularly horrible. We attempt to balance honest depictions of the past with sensitivity toward the needs of a young audience. Thus, details about some of the more shocking actions of certain Roman emperors, like Nero and Caligula, are muted.

UNIT 21

FALL OF ROME

This Week's Quest

Learn how the western part of the Roman Empire met its end, and how the eastern part of the empire kept on going strong for quite some time.

Resources & Materials

History Quest: Early Times (HQ)

Usborne Encyclopedia of World History with Internet Links (UEWH)

Map 9 (Appendix C)

History Travel Log page and The Visigoth illustration (Appendix C)

Roman Numerals page (Appendix C)

Supplies Needed for Day 3

- Index cards, preferably colored
- Markers or decorative tape (e.g. washi tape)
- Scissors
- Poster board
- Glue
- Card stock or other thick paper
- Paper fastener/brad

Enrichment Reading

Roman Diary: The Journal of Iliona, Young Slave by Richard Platt

Unit Schedule

Day 1 Discover	Day 2 Explore	Day 3 Create	Day 4 Demonstrate	Day 5 Enrich
UEWH pages 192–195	History Hop! The Visigoth	Make a Roman Numeral Clock	Review Terms & Concepts	Explore Pandia Web Links
HQ Chapter 21 Fall of Rome	History Travel Log		Complete one or more review options	Read from Enrichment Reading list
Map 9				

Terms & Concepts

The Big Ideas

- During the Pax Romana, life was good for many Romans. After the Pax Romana, regular people in the Roman Empire had trouble finding jobs and having enough money to take care of their families. They also had to pay high taxes.
- The Visigoths were a barbarian group that was allowed to come inside the borders of the Roman Empire. Although Visigoths helped the Roman army, Romans did not treat the Visigoths well. So the Visigoths began fighting against the Romans.
- The king of the Visigoths, Alaric, led his people in sacking (attacking, invading, and taking wealth) the city of Rome. Another group called the Vandals also sacked Rome.

The Details

- The emperor Diocletian tried to solve some of Rome's problems by splitting the Roman Empire in half so that each half would be easier to govern.
- Emperor Constantine made a law that everyone in the Roman Empire could follow whatever religion they wanted. Soon after, Christianity became the official religion of the Roman Empire.
- The Roman Empire was so big that it was hard to hire enough soldiers to guard all of the borders. Roman emperors had to spend more and more money on soldiers, which meant they had less to spend on things like repairing roads and building aqueducts.

Lessons

Day 1. Discover

- ☐ **Read pages 192–195 in UEWH.** If desired, navigate to some of the websites recommended in the book.
- ☐ **Read Chapter 21: Fall of Rome in HQ pages 373–382**
- ☐ **Complete Map 9.** Referring to the map in HQ on page 377:

1. Label these bodies of water:

   Mediterranean Sea
   Black Sea
   Atlantic Ocean
   Danube River

2. Label these countries:

   TURKEY
   SPAIN
   FRANCE
   BULGARIA
   ENGLAND
   MOROCCO
   ALGERIA
   ITALY
   GREECE

3. Label these cities:

   •Byzantium (Constantinople)
   •Rome

4. Shade the two different sides of the Roman Empire in two colors.

Day 2. Explore

- ☐ **Read History Hop! The Visigoth in HQ pages 383–390**
- ☐ **History Travel Log.** Complete the travel log page for this unit and place it in your history notebook.

Day 3. Create

- ☐ **Craft: Make a Roman Numeral Clock**

Supplies:

- Roman Numerals page (Appendix C)
- Markers or decorative tape (e.g. washi tape)
- Six 3x5 plain index cards, cut in half crosswise, preferably colored
- Scissors
- Piece of poster board
- Glue
- Card stock or other thick paper to make the minute and hour hands
- Paper fastener/brad

Directions:

Use the Roman Numerals page as a model to draw a Roman numeral on each card. If you would like fancier numerals, you could use washi tape instead of markers to make the numerals. Arrange the numeral cards onto the poster board in the shape of a round clock face and glue into place. Design and cut out your longer minute hand and your shorter second hand. Attach them to the center of the circle with a paper fastener. Once your child is comfortable with the Roman numerals, they can also use the clock face to practice telling time.

Day 4. Demonstrate

- ☐ **Read through the Terms & Concepts.** Optional: Copy some or all of the Terms & Concepts into your history notebook.
- ☐ **Complete one or more of the following** in order to strengthen your child's knowledge of the material and to provide an opportunity for you to evaluate their understanding:

Option #1 Short Answers

Answer the following questions verbally or write them in your history notebook:

Q: What is term means the 200-year period where life was good for many Romans?
A: *This was the Pax Romana.*

Q: What did the Romans call the people who lived outside the Roman Empire?
A: *People from outside the empire were called barbarians.*

Q: What religion did the emperor Constantine convert to?
A: *Constantine converted to Christianity.*

Option #2 Narration

Answer the following verbally or in writing:

- List three important things you learned about the fall of Rome.

Option #3 Copywork

Copy or write from dictation one of the following into your history notebook:

> The Roman Empire fell after outside groups called barbarians attacked.

> The Roman Empire fell because it had many problems. It was running out of money and outside groups, like the Visigoths, attacked it.

Day 5. Enrich

- ☐ **Visit www.pandiapress.com/weblinks.** There you will find a description of some recommended websites related to this unit.

- ☐ **Read from the Enrichment Reading list**

  Roman Diary: The Journal of Iliona, Young Slave by Richard Platt. This book, presented as a diary of a young Greek girl captured by pirates and sold to be a Roman slave, takes place around the year 100 CE, but much of the material applies to Roman reality in the later period of the Empire. While fictional, Platt covers an admirable number of topics in a detailed and compelling way. While the story gives Iliona a relatively easy lot as a slave, and ends fairly happily, it does not shy away from some of the darker aspects of slavery and Roman life in general. Parents should consider reviewing before using, but in terms of quality, this book is recommended.

Unit Notes

UNIT 22

KUSHITES AND AKSUMITES

This Week's Quest

Learn about the ancient African kingdoms of Kush and Aksum, and how they became strong civilizations through trade.

Resources & Materials

History Quest: Early Times (HQ)

Usborne Encyclopedia of World History with Internet Links (UEWH)

Map 10 (Appendix C)

History Travel Log page and The Merchants illustration (Appendix C)

Supplies Needed for Day 3

- Egg carton
- Bowls
- Small play pieces (e.g. pebbles, pennies, buttons)

Enrichment Reading

African Beginnings by James Haskins

Unit Schedule

Day 1 Discover	Day 2 Explore	Day 3 Create	Day 4 Demonstrate	Day 5 Enrich
UEWH pages 172–173	History Hop! The Merchants	Make a Mancala Game	Review Terms & Concepts	Explore Pandia Web Links
HQ Chapter 22 Kushites and Aksumites	Google Earth		Complete one or more review options	Read from Enrichment Reading list
Map 10	History Travel Log			

Terms & Concepts

The Big Ideas

- Kush was an ancient African civilization. The Kushites increased their power by moving their capital city to a place where they were able to make iron weapons and tools.
- The powerful African kingdom of Aksum was able to conquer the Kushites because the Kushites were running out of resources.
- The Aksumite city of Adulis became an important trading city. Merchants sailed across the Indian Ocean to trade goods such as salt. Merchants also traveled through the desert with caravans—groups of camels and their drivers.

The Details

- In ancient Kush, women had more power than in most other ancient civilizations. Kushite queens, called kandakes, sometimes ruled. A kandake named Amanirenas protected her people from being conquered by the Romans.
- When the Roman Empire fell, Aksum got weaker because the Aksumites depended on the Romans as a trading partner.

Lessons

Day 1. Discover

- ☐ **Read pages 172–173 in UEWH.** If desired, navigate to some of the websites recommended in the book.
- ☐ **Read Chapter 22: Kushites and Aksumites in HQ pages 391–400**
- ☐ **Complete Map 10.** Referring to the map in HQ on page 394:

1. Label these bodies of water and desert:

   Nile River
   Red Sea
   Mediterranean Sea
   Indian Ocean
   Sahara

2. Label these countries/regions:

   EGYPT
   NUBIA
   ARABIA
   KUSH
   AKSUM

3. Label these cities:

   •Napata
   •Meroe
   •Adulis

4. Shade the areas of Kush and Aksum in two different colors.

Day 2. Explore

- ☐ **Read History Hop! The Merchants in HQ pages 401–411**
- ☐ **Google Earth.** Search for "Pyramids of Meroe, Sudan" to see this Kushite architecture.
- ☐ **History Travel Log.** Complete the travel log page for this unit and place it in your history notebook.

Day 3. Create

☐ **Craft: Make a Mancala Game**

Supplies:

- Egg carton
- 2 bowls
- 48 small play pieces (pebbles, marbles, dried beans, buttons, beads, etc.)
- Alternate Option: If you would like to own a Mancala set for your family to enjoy, you can find several options online, generally for under $20.

Mancala is a game that was invented in the region of Africa we've been studying in ancient times. There are many variations on game play. This is a fairly simple version to learn.

Directions:

Cut the lid off of an egg carton. Place a bowl at each end. The bowl set on the right side of each opponent is called their "well."

To Play:

Fill each of the 12 cups with four of the play pieces. When it's your turn, take all of the play pieces out of any of the six cups on your side. Moving counterclockwise, put one piece into each of the succeeding cups and your well. If you have more pieces left after dropping one in your well, continue by dropping those pieces one by one into your opponent's cups until you have run out of pieces. Your opponent then takes all of the play pieces out of one of the cups on their side. They place one piece into each of their succeeding cups and their well. If your final play piece lands in your own well, you get to take another turn. If your final play piece ends up in an empty cup on either side, you can take all of the play pieces in your opponent's well and put them in your own well. Play continues this way. However, make sure that each player skips their opponent's well. Play continues until all of the play pieces end up in the two wells. The player with the most pieces in their own well wins. Again, this is just one variation of the game—there are many other ways to play.

Day 4. Demonstrate

- ☐ **Read through the Terms & Concepts.** Optional: Copy some or all of the Terms & Concepts into your history notebook.
- ☐ **Complete one or more of the following** in order to strengthen your child's knowledge of the material and to provide an opportunity for you to evaluate their understanding:

Option #1 Short Answers

Answer the following questions verbally or write them in your history notebook:

Q: What were the tools and weapons made of that the Kushites sold to other civilizations?
A: They were made of iron.

Q: What is a kandake?
A: A kandake is the name for a queen in the Kushite kingdom.

Q: Who conquered the Kushites when they began to run out of resources?
A: The Aksumites conquered the Kushites.

Q: Which ocean did merchants cross to get to the important trading city of Adulis?
A: They crossed the Indian Ocean.

Option #2 Narration

Answer the following verbally or in writing:

- List three important things you learned about the Kushites and the Aksumites.

Option #3 Copywork

Copy or write from dictation one of the following into your history notebook:

> The kingdom of Aksum in Africa was very good at trading with other civilizations.

The kingdom of Kush was an ancient African civilization south of Egypt. After it grew weak, the kingdom of Aksum conquered it. Aksumites traded with other civilizations. Merchants traveled to Aksum through the desert on camels.

Day 5. Enrich

☐ **Visit www.pandiapress.com/weblinks.** There you will find a description of some recommended websites related to this unit.

☐ **Read from the Enrichment Reading list**

African Beginnings by James Haskins. Most children's books on ancient Africa move well beyond ancient times. But you can focus on the appropriate chapters in Haskins's book, which is well-written and beautifully illustrated.

Children's books that focus on ancient times in Africa (other than Egypt) are hard, if not impossible, to find. Some of this has to do with relative dearth of historical documents from this time period. Some has to do with the fact that most African civilizations developed later than civilizations elsewhere, like in Mesopotamia. There is much more children's material on African developments and stories in the era beginning after ancient times.

Unit Notes

UNIT 23

CHINA: PART ONE

This Week's Quest

Learn about ancient China, land of ruling dynasties, warring groups, and some of the finest cloth created in the ancient world.

Resources & Materials

History Quest: Early Times (HQ)

Usborne Encyclopedia of World History with Internet Links (UEWH)

Map 11 (Appendix C)

History Travel Log page and The Silk Mother illustration (Appendix C)

Supplies Needed for Day 3

- Craft sticks
- Black marker
- Scissors
- String

Enrichment Reading

Fa Mulan: The Story of a Woman Warrior by Robert D. San Souci

Liu and the Bird: A Journey in Chinese Calligraphy by Catherine Louis

Unit Schedule

Day 1 Discover	Day 2 Explore	Day 3 Create	Day 4 Demonstrate	Day 5 Enrich
UEWH pages 164–165	History Hop! The Silk Mother	Make an Ancient Chinese Book	Review Terms & Concepts	Explore Pandia Web Links
HQ Chapter 23 China: Part One	History Travel Log		Complete one or more review options	Read from Enrichment Reading list
Map 11				

Terms & Concepts

The Big Ideas

❋ Two famous ruling families, or dynasties, in ancient China were the Shang Dynasty and the Zhou Dynasty.

❋ One of the most important goods the Chinese traded was silk, which could only be produced in China for many hundreds of years.

❋ Confucius was a great Chinese philosopher who tried to teach people how to live well together.

The Details

❋ Ancient Chinese people believed that ancestor spirits had great power and should be respected.

❋ China was very far away from other wealthy ancient civilizations, like the Egyptians or Romans. So, it took much longer for China to become involved in trade beyond its borders.

❋ Two rivers that were important to Chinese civilization were the Yellow River in the north and the Yangtze River in the south.

Lessons

Day 1. Discover

- ☐ **Read pages 164–165 in UEWH.** If desired, navigate to some of the websites recommended in the book.
- ☐ **Read Chapter 23: China: Part One in HQ pages 413–422**
- ☐ **Complete Map 11.** Referring to the map in HQ on page 415:

1. Label these bodies of water:

   Mediterranean Sea
   Pacific Ocean
   Indian Ocean
   Yangtze River
   Yellow River

2. Label these countries/regions:

   EGYPT
   PERSIA
   INDIA
   CHINA
   ARABIA
   MESOPOTAMIA

3. Draw triangles to indicate the location of the Himalayas.

Day 2. Explore

- ☐ **Read History Hop! The Silk Mother in HQ pages 423–429**
- ☐ **History Travel Log.** Complete the travel log page for this unit and place it in your history notebook.

Day 3. Create

☐ **Craft: Make an Ancient Chinese Book**

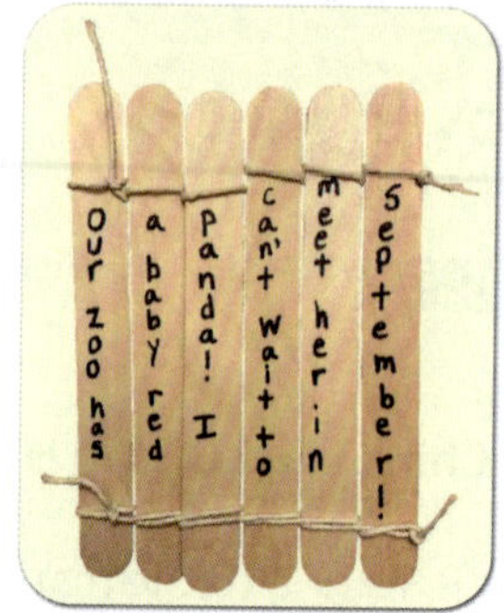

Supplies:

- 5–10 craft sticks
- Black marker
- Scissors
- String

Directions:

Encourage your child to come up with one or two sentences to write in their book. Write the first few words on the first stick, from top to bottom, rather than left to right. Continue onto the second stick, and so on. When writing, avoid the top and bottom quarters of the stick so the words don't get covered when you tie the sticks together. When you're finished writing the sentence(s), cut a length of string and tie a knot around the first stick about ¼ of the way down. Wrap the string around the second stick, also ¼ of the way down, and so on. Tie a knot around the final stick. Repeat the same process with a second piece of string near the bottom of the "book," about ¾ of the way down the sticks.

As an alternative, search for Chinese symbols online or in a book. Copy chosen symbols and write down the English word corresponding to each symbol underneath.

Day 4. Demonstrate

☐ **Read through the Terms & Concepts.** Optional: Copy some or all of the Terms & Concepts into your history notebook.

☐ **Complete one or more of the following** in order to strengthen your child's knowledge of the material and to provide an opportunity for you to evaluate their understanding:

Option #1 Short Answers

Answer the following questions verbally or write them in your history notebook:

Q: Who were two of the most famous ruling families in ancient China?
A: *The Shang Dynasty and the Zhou Dynasty were famous ruling families.*

Q: What did the Chinese use to make silk cloth?
A: *They used the cocoon of the silkworm to make silk.*

Q: Who in ancient China came up with a system for how people should treat each other?

A: *Confucius created this system.*

Q: What did the ancient Chinese people believe about their ancestors?

A: *They believed that the spirits of their ancestors had great power and should be respected.*

Option #2 Narration

Answer the following verbally or in writing:

- List three important things you learned about ancient Chinese civilization.

Option #3 Copywork

Copy or write from dictation one of the following into your history notebook:

China was ruled by different dynasties, including the Shang and the Zhou.

Ancient China was ruled by different dynasties. One of the longest ruling dynasties was the Zhou Dynasty. After the Zhou Dynasty became weaker, ancient China was broken up into many different warring parts. A great Chinese philosopher named Confucius lived during this Warring States Period.

Day 5. Enrich

- ☐ **Visit www.pandiapress.com/weblinks.** There you will find a description of some recommended websites related to this unit.
- ☐ **Read from the Enrichment Reading list**

  Fa Mulan: The Story of a Woman Warrior by Robert D. San Souci. This beautifully illustrated book tells the legend of Mulan, a woman who fought during ancient Chinese history.

  Liu and the Bird: A Journey in Chinese Calligraphy by Catherine Louis. While not a historical book per se, this volume teaches children about the evolution of Chinese writing in an engaging way.

Unit Notes

UNIT 24

CHINA: PART TWO

This Week's Quest

Learn about the first emperor of all of China and an amazing underground army made of terracotta.

Resources & Materials

History Quest: Early Times (HQ)

Usborne Encyclopedia of World History with Internet Links (UEWH)

History Travel Log page and The Scholar illustration (Appendix C)

Enrichment Reading

Hidden Army: Clay Soldiers of Ancient China by Jane O'Connor

The Emperor Who Built the Great Wall by Jillian Lin

The Girl Who Became Emperor by Jillian Lin

Supplies Needed for Day 3

- Broth
- Soy sauce
- Rice or white vinegar
- Honey or other sweetener
- Protein of your choice
- Cornstarch
- Salt
- Cooking oil
- Large pan or wok, and cooking utensils
- Vegetables: onion, broccoli, carrots, red bell pepper
- Garlic
- Rice

Unit Schedule

Day 1 **Discover**	Day 2 **Explore**	Day 3 **Create**	Day 4 **Demonstrate**	Day 5 **Enrich**
UEWH pages 166–169	History Hop! The Scholar	Make Chinese Stir-Fry	Review Terms & Concepts	Explore Pandia Web Links
HQ Chapter 24 China: Part Two	Google Earth		Complete one or more review options	Read from Enrichment Reading list
	History Travel Log			

Terms & Concepts

The Big Ideas

- King Zheng of the state of Qin became the ruler of all of China in 221 BCE. He gave himself the title of emperor and became known as Qin Shi Huangdi, or First Emperor from Qin.
- Qin Shi Huangdi was a harsh ruler but he did unify the country. He also ordered that the Terracotta Army be made to protect his spirit from enemies after he died.
- The Han Dynasty began to rule China after the Qin Dynasty ended. Leaders of the Han Dynasty built a great capital city, better roads, and improved trade in China.

The Details

- Confucianism became very important in ancient China from the beginning of the Han Dynasty.
- The religion of Buddhism became very important in ancient China by the end of the Han Dynasty.
- Paper was invented in ancient China around the year 100 CE.

Lessons

Day 1. Discover

- ☐ **Read pages 166–169 in UEWH.** If desired, navigate to some of the websites recommended in the book.
- ☐ **Read Chapter 24: China: Part Two in HQ pages 431–441**

Day 2. Explore

- ☐ **Read History Hop! The Scholar in HQ pages 442–450**
- ☐ **Google Earth.** Search for "Emperor Qinshihuang's Mausoleum Site Museum" to get a closer look at the Terracotta Army.
- ☐ **History Travel Log.** Complete the travel log page for this unit and place it in your history notebook.

Day 3. Create

- ☐ **Cooking: Make Chinese Stir-Fry**

Supplies:

- ½ cup vegetable or chicken broth (low sodium)
- ¼ cup soy sauce, regular or low sodium
- 1 tablespoon rice wine or white vinegar
- 2 teaspoons honey, sugar, or vegan sweetener of your choice
- 2 tablespoons cornstarch
- ½ teaspoon salt
- 2–3 tablespoons cooking oil
- ½ medium onion
- 2 cups broccoli florets
- 2 medium carrots, peeled and sliced thinly
- ½ medium red bell pepper, sliced
- 2 cloves garlic, minced or crushed
- 3 cups prepared rice
- Optional: chopsticks
- 1 pound protein (thinly sliced flank steak, pork loin, chicken breast, or package of extra firm tofu). If using tofu, press extra liquid out of the block of tofu by wrapping a tea towel around it and placing a weight, such as a heavy pot, on top of it for about an hour.

Directions:

Whisk together broth, soy sauce, vinegar, and sweetener. Set aside. In a plastic bag or bowl, toss protein with corn starch and salt. Heat oil in a heavy-bottom skillet or wok. Stir-fry the coated protein until browned. Add vegetables and stir-fry for another two minutes, making sure not to let the garlic burn. Add sauce mixture and stir until protein is cooked through and vegetables are as soft as you want them. Adjust seasoning to your taste. Serve with prepared rice. If desired, eat with chopsticks!

Day 4. Demonstrate

- ☐ **Read through the Terms & Concepts.** Optional: Copy some or all of the Terms & Concepts into your history notebook.
- ☐ **Complete one or more of the following** in order to strengthen your child's knowledge of the material and to provide an opportunity for you to evaluate their understanding:

Option #1 Short Answers

Answer the following questions verbally or write them in your history notebook:

Q: What kind of ruler was Qin Shi Huangdi?
A: Qin Shi Huangdi was a harsh ruler with strict rules.

Q: What amazing thing did Shi Huangdi build to protect himself after he died?
A: He built an army of terracotta soldiers.

Q: What important invention did the ancient Chinese invent around the year 100 CE?
A: They invented paper.

Q: Which two religions became important in China during the Han Dynasty?
A: Buddhism and Confucianism became important religions.

Option #2 Narration

Answer the following verbally or in writing:

- List three important things you learned about ancient Chinese civilization.

Option #3 Copywork/Dictation

Copy or write from dictation one of the following into your history notebook:

Shi Huangdi was the first emperor of all of China.

Qin Shi Huangdi was the first emperor of all of China. He was a harsh ruler but he made some good changes to the country. The Han Dynasty took over next. Han leaders made China stronger and wealthier.

Day 5. Enrich

- ☐ **Visit www.pandiapress.com/weblinks.** There you will find a description of some recommended websites related to this unit.
- ☐ **Read one or more from the Enrichment Reading list**

  Hidden Army: Clay Soldiers of Ancient China by Jane O'Connor. Simple storytelling and photographs explain the story of the terracotta soldiers and their discovery.

  The Emperor Who Built the Great Wall by Jillian Lin. Colorful, interesting illustrations are a highlight of this well-told overview of the emperor of a Qin Dynasty.

  The Girl Who Became Emperor by Jillian Lin. A beautifully illustrated book from noted children's author Jillian Lin, telling the true story of a seventh-century Chinese empress.

Unit Notes

HYGGE HISTORY #4

CHINESE MYTHOLOGY

This Week's Quest

- Read and enjoy Chinese mythology.

Resources

Chinese Children's Favorite Stories by Mingmei Yip (ISBN 978-0804850179)

or choose any number of the following by Li Jian,

- *The Water Dragon: A Chinese Legend* (ISBN 978-1602209787)
- *The Snake Goddess Colors the World* (ISBN 978-1602209824)
- *The Horse and the Mysterious Drawing* (ISBN 978-1602209848)
- *The Sheep Beauty* (ISBN 978-1602209886)
- *The Little Monkey King's Journey* (ISBN 978-1602209817)
- *The Magical Rooster* (ISBN 978-1602209954)
- *The Bronze Dog* (ISBN 978-1602209985)
- *The Little Pigs and the Sweet Rice Cakes* (ISBN 978-1602204539)
- *The Little Rat and the Golden Seed* (ISBN: 978-1602204591)

Hygge History

So far, all of our literature selections from ancient times have been epics—grand, sweeping tales of heroic deeds, fate, love, friendship, and thrilling battles. This week, however, there will be no epic drama, because the ancient Chinese didn't focus on epics. The most famous writings of ancient China were actually much more about philosophy. Unfortunately, there just aren't any gorgeously illustrated, readily available, kid-friendly versions of Confucian philosophy or *The Art of War*.

Instead, this week we have two delightful options in the folk-tale genre:

Option 1: *Chinese Children's Favorite Stories* retold and illustrated by Mingmei Yip

The thirteen Chinese tales and legends in this collection don't all have ancient roots, but the topics covered, the excellent writing, and the lovely traditional illustrations make this a solid choice for young students learning about ancient China. Astute readers will notice a story about the qin, a stringed instrument that appears briefly in *History Quest's* History Hop: The Silk Mother.

Option 2: *Stories of the Chinese Zodiac* series by Li Jian

According to Chinese legends, Qin Shi Huangdi (famous for his Terracotta Army, among other things) is also the inventor of the Chinese lunar calendar, which led to the creation of the Chinese zodiac. The Chinese zodiac came into use in ancient times and is still popular today. Li Jian's series based on the zodiac includes a story and lovely ink illustrations for each animal. The stories are printed in both English and Chinese characters. Although there are twelve animals in the Chinese zodiac, this is a fairly new series and only nine books are available as of early 2019. Please do not feel compelled to purchase all of these books, which would run over $100! They should be readily available to borrow from most major public library systems.

Hygge History Notes

UNIT 25

BYZANTINE EMPIRE

This Week's Quest

Learn what happened to the area of Rome that kept on going after the western part failed, partly thanks to a strong emperor and an equally strong empress.

Resources & Materials

History Quest: Early Times (HQ)

Usborne Encyclopedia of World History with Internet Links (UEWH)

Map 12 (Appendix C)

History Travel Log page and The Circus Performer illustration (Appendix C)

Supplies Needed for Day 3

- Eggshells
- Paints and paintbrushes
- Pencil
- Glue
- Card stock

Enrichment Reading

The Silk Route: 7,000 Miles of History by John S. Major

Unit Schedule

Day 1 Discover	Day 2 Explore	Day 3 Create	Day 4 Demonstrate	Day 5 Enrich
UEWH pages 202–203	History Hop! The Circus Performer	Make an Eggshell Byzantine Mosaic	Review Terms & Concepts	Explore Pandia Web Links
HQ Chapter 25 Byzantine Empire	Google Earth		Complete one or more review options	Read from Enrichment Reading list
Map 12	History Travel Log			

Terms & Concepts

The Big Ideas

- The Roman Emperor Constantine moved the capital of the empire to a city called Constantinople. The eastern part of the Roman Empire now became known as the Byzantine Empire.
- Justinian was one of the greatest emperors of the Byzantine Empire. His wife, Theodora, helped rule as empress. Theodora grew up in a circus-performing family.
- Justinian built a beautiful church called the Hagia Sophia.

The Details

- Justinian and Theodora had to face the Nika Riots, when many people in the Byzantine Empire rose up against them. They ended up winning.
- Justinian's general, Belisarius, won many battles in the west to regain parts of the Roman Empire for Justinian, but Justinian stopped trusting him and Belisarius had to stop.
- People in the Byzantine Empire loved watching the sport of chariot racing.

Lessons

Day 1. Discover

- ☐ **Read pages 202–203 in UEWH.** If desired, navigate to some of the websites recommended in the book.
- ☐ **Read Chapter 25: Byzantine Empire in HQ pages 451–460**
- ☐ **Complete Map 12.** Referring to the map in HQ on page 454:

1. Label these bodies of water:

   Atlantic Ocean
   Black Sea
   Mediterranean Sea

2. Label these regions:

   AFRICA
   EGYPT
   ARABIA
   GREECE
   ITALY

3. Label these kingdoms:

   Kingdom of the Visigoths
   Kingdom of the Ostragoths
   Kingdom of the Vandals

4. Label these cities:

   •Carthage
   •Jerusalem
   •Constantinople
   •Rome

5. Shade the Byzantine Empire under Justinian.

Day 2. Explore

- ☐ **Read History Hop! The Circus Performer in HQ pages 461–470**
- ☐ **Google Earth.** Search for "Hagia Sophia Museum" to learn more about Emperor Justinian's most famous architectural project.
- ☐ **History Travel Log.** Complete the travel log page for this unit and place it in your history notebook.

Day 3. Create

☐ **Craft: Make an Eggshell Byzantine Mosaic**

Detail of the mosaics of Justinian and Theodora, 527 CE

Supplies:

- 3–8 eggshells, washed and set aside to dry (fewer if you plan to make a smaller mosaic, more if you want a larger one)
- Paints (Byzantine artists used golds, blues, greens, and oranges a lot, so consider emphasizing these colors if you want to make a Byzantine-style mosaic.)
- Paintbrush
- Pencil
- Glue
- Card stock or thin piece of cardboard (because of the challenging nature of this project, don't use too large a piece of paper or cardboard)

Directions:

When the washed eggshells are dry, paint the outsides with the colors of your choice. Set aside to dry again. Draw a simple picture with large spaces onto your piece of card stock. For an extra challenge or for older students, aim to make a picture like Justinian and Theodora's famous mosaic, complete with fancy hats. When the painted eggshells are dry, break them into smaller pieces. Paint a section of your paper with a layer of glue. Gently press eggshell pieces onto the glue. If they crack, that's fine! Repeat until the picture is complete.

Day 4. Demonstrate

- ☐ **Read through the Terms & Concepts.** Optional: Copy some or all of the Terms & Concepts into your history notebook.
- ☐ **Complete one or more of the following** in order to strengthen your child's knowledge of the material and to provide an opportunity for you to evaluate their understanding:

Option #1 Short Answers

Answer the following questions verbally or write them in your history notebook:

Q: Where did Constantine move the capital of the Roman Empire?
A: He moved it to Byzantium (later called Constantinople).

Q: What is the name of the most famous Byzantine emperor?
A: The most famous Byzantine emperor was Justinian.

Q: What was Theodora's childhood like?
A: She was a performer with the circus before becoming empress.

Q: What sport did people of the Byzantine Empire love to watch?
A: They loved chariot racing.

Option #2 Narration

Answer the following verbally or in writing:

- List three important things you learned about Byzantine Empire.

Option #3 Copywork

Copy or write from dictation one of the following into your history notebook:

> Justinian and Theodora stopped the Nika Riots and built beautiful buildings, like the Hagia Sophia.

The Byzantine Empire was the eastern part of the Roman Empire. Justinian and Theodora were some of its best leaders. They stopped the Nika Riots and built beautiful buildings, like the Hagia Sophia.

Day 5. Enrich

- ☐ **Visit www.pandiapress.com/weblinks.** There you will find a description of some recommended websites related to this unit.
- ☐ **Read from the Enrichment Reading list**

  The Silk Route: 7,000 Miles of History by John S. Major. This excellently illustrated book discusses the trade routes through China into the Byzantine Empire.

Unit Notes

UNIT 26

ARABIA

This Week's Quest

Learn about the Arabs and the beginnings of the religion of Islam and the Islamic Empire.

Resources & Materials

History Quest: Early Times (HQ)

Usborne Encyclopedia of World History with Internet Links (UEWH)

Map 13 (Appendix C)

History Travel Log page and The Caliph illustration (Appendix C)

Supplies Needed for Day 3

- Rice
- Salt
- Broth
- Butter
- Milk
- Cooking utensils

Enrichment Reading

1001 Inventions & Awesome Facts from Muslim Civilization by National Geographic

Unit Schedule

Day 1 Discover	Day 2 Explore	Day 3 Create	Day 4 Demonstrate	Day 5 Enrich
UEWH pages 171, 206–207	History Hop! The Caliph	Make Saleeg	Review Terms & Concepts	Explore Pandia Web Links
HQ Chapter 26 Arabia	History Travel Log		Complete one or more review options	Read from Enrichment Reading list
Map 13				

Terms & Concepts

The Big Ideas

❋ The ancient Arabs lived on a large piece of land between the Persian Gulf and the Red Sea. Many of the ancient Arabs were nomads who organized in clans and tribes, not in a single kingdom.

❋ Muhammad was an Arab who introduced a new religion called Islam. People who believe in Islam are called Muslims. They believe in one god called Allah and follow the teachings in a book called the Koran.

❋ Muhammad conquered all of the Arabian peninsula. After Muhammad died, other Muslim leaders called caliphs conquered even more territory, creating the Islamic Empire.

The Details

❋ Muhammad's teachings about Islam were at first rejected in his birth city of Mecca, so he moved to another Arabian city called Medina.

❋ Muslims took over much of the land that used to be controlled by the old Roman Empire, including all of North Africa and Spain.

Lessons

Day 1. Discover

- ☐ **Read pages 171 and 206–207 in UEWH.** If desired, navigate to some of the websites recommended in the book.
- ☐ **Read Chapter 26: Arabia in HQ pages 471–482**
- ☐ **Complete Map 13.** Referring to the map in HQ on page 473:

1. Label these bodies of water:

   Strait of Gibraltar
   Mediterranean Sea
   Red Sea
   Arabian Sea
   Persian Gulf

2. Label this country:

   SPAIN

3. Label this area:

   Arabian Peninsula

4. Label these cities:

   •Constantinople
   •Damascus
   •Medina
   •Mecca
   •Adulis

5. Shade the extent of the Islamic Empire at its greatest.

 Day 2. Explore

☐ **Read History Hop! The Caliph in HQ pages 483–490**

☐ **History Travel Log.** Complete the travel log page for this unit and place it in your history notebook.

 Day 3. Create

☐ **Cooking: Make Saleeg**

Supplies:

- 1½ cups long grain rice
- 1 teaspoon salt
- 3 cups low sodium broth (chicken broth is traditional for this recipe, but you could also use vegetable broth or vegetarian "no-chicken" broth)
- ¼ cup butter or vegan alternative
- 1½ cups milk, preferably whole milk (For a vegan option, choose a rich non-dairy milk such as coconut milk or oat milk.)

Directions:

Combine rice, salt, broth, and butter in a pot. Bring to a boil and reduce heat to low, stirring occasionally, until rice is very soft. Add extra broth if needed. Once soft, add the milk and continue cooking, stirring frequently, until a porridge-like consistency is reached.

This recipe also works great in an electric pressure cooker. Reduce the broth to 1½ cups if you use a pressure cooker. Set valve to sealing and use the manual pressure cook setting for 4 minutes. Perform a 10-minute natural release and then change to the sauté setting on low in order to finish cooking with the milk.

 Day 4. Demonstrate

☐ **Read through the Terms & Concepts.** Optional: Copy some or all of the Terms & Concepts into your history notebook.

☐ **Complete one or more of the following** in order to strengthen your child's knowledge of the material and to provide an opportunity for you to evaluate their understanding:

Option #1 Short Answers

Answer the following questions verbally or write them in your history notebook:

Q: What religion did Muhammad introduce, and what are the followers of this religion called?
A: *He founded Islam, and the followers of Islam are called Muslims.*

Q: Why did Muhammad leave his home city of Mecca and where did he go?
A: *People did not accept the beliefs of Islam in Mecca at first, so Muhammad went to Medina.*

Q: How did the earliest Muslims treat the people that they conquered who didn't believe in Islam?
A: *They let them follow their own religions, but they had to pay a tax to the Islamic Empire.*

Option #2 Narration

Answer the following verbally or in writing:

- List three important things you learned about the Islamic Empire.

Option #3 Copywork

Copy or write from dictation one of the following into your history notebook:

Muhammad founded the religion of Islam in the Arabian peninsula.

The Arabs were an ancient people who believed in many gods and lived in the Arabian peninsula. But then a man named Muhammad taught them the religion of Islam and most of them became Muslims. The Muslims conquered a lot of land.

Day 5. Enrich

- ☐ **Visit www.pandiapress.com/weblinks.** There you will find a description of some recommended websites related to this unit.
- ☐ **Read from the Enrichment Reading list**

  1001 Inventions & Awesome Facts from Muslim Civilization by National Geographic. Full of Information and pictures, this book covers a much wider range of time than is covered in this unit.

Unit Notes

UNIT 27

CONCLUSION

This Week's Quest

Think back on what you learned this year about ancient history. Think about what you'd like to study in the future.

Resources & Materials

History Quest: Early Times (HQ)

Usborne Encyclopedia of World History with Internet Links (UEWH)

Completed History Travel Log

This last unit is a good opportunity to circle back to anything you may have missed or did not finish this year. Did you have to skip a craft because you realized too late that you didn't have empty paper towel rolls, a cork, or some other material? Were you unable to read the last chapters of any of the hygge history books? Do you still have some (perhaps now overdue) library books you didn't get to? Now would be a good time to take a look at any missed or incomplete projects and books and either work on them this week, or put them on a to-do list for rainy afternoons in the summer when you're looking for something to do. We've also provided a few extra possible activities to do this week as you say goodbye (for now) to humankind's early times and prepare to enter the middle times.

Conclusion Activities

1. *History Quest* Conclusion

☐ **Read the Conclusion in HQ pages 491–498**

2. Take a Walk Down Memory Lane

By this time, your child should have completed their History Travel Log based on the History Hop sections of *History Quest*. Take a look through the travel log together and think about the fascinating people from ancient times you met this year. Questions for discussion:

- Who was your favorite person to meet? Why?
- If you had to live in one of these ancient civilizations in history, which one would you pick and why?
- You met lots of ancient people with very different jobs—author, sailor, toolmaker, scribe, ironworker, artisan, engineer, general, city planner, queen, pharaoh, embalmer, and more. Which ancient career do you think you would like? Which ancient job would you rather avoid?

3. What's Your Angle?

Some historians develop a special interest in a particular aspect of history. They might even become an expert in that one particular topic. For example, one historian might be really interested in the history of theatrical performance, studying how live theatre has developed and changed from ancient Greek tragedies all the way through New York's Broadway shows. Another historian might be interested in battle strategy. They might study famous battles from ancient times all the way up through World War II's D-Day and beyond. Other historians might be interested in the history of aspects of everyday life like food, clothing, housing, or what people did for fun in their spare time.

As your child wraps up their study of ancient times, encourage them to give some thought to what specific aspects of history study might blossom into areas of interest…or who knows, maybe even a future career opportunity! One way to begin a discussion about this is to take a look at the illustrations from the "Ancient World" section of UEWH. (Don't forget the Paleolithic folks who appear on the few pages prior to the start of the "Ancient World" section. Also, a couple of the chapters covered at the very end of *History Quest* appear in the earliest pages of the "Medieval World" section of UEWH, so take a look at those as well.) Have your child choose one aspect of history to "track" over time by flipping through the pages of illustrations and pointing out changes over time. Some possible options to consider:

- Clothing–What did the clothing look like during Paleolithic times? How about in the Indus Valley, in Crete, or in Persia?
- Architecture–What types of structures did people build in hunter-gatherer societies of the Paleolithic era? What did houses look like during the Han Dynasty? How about the buildings of Babylon or the Byzantine Empire?
- Transportation and travel–How do the earliest boats compare to the boats of the Nile Valley? What about Phoenician trading ships? Persian and Greek ships? How do the walking trails and roadways from Ancient India, Roman Empire, Catal Huyuk, Mohenjo-daro, and others compare? What were the different modes of transportation for people in ancient times?

Your child might show a spark of interest in one of these topics or in another topic altogether. If you have time in your schedule before starting your study of medieval times—perhaps over the summer—you can help your child dig deeper into their area of interest with library books, documentaries, field trips, and/or online resources.

APPENDIX A: MAP KEYS

Map 1

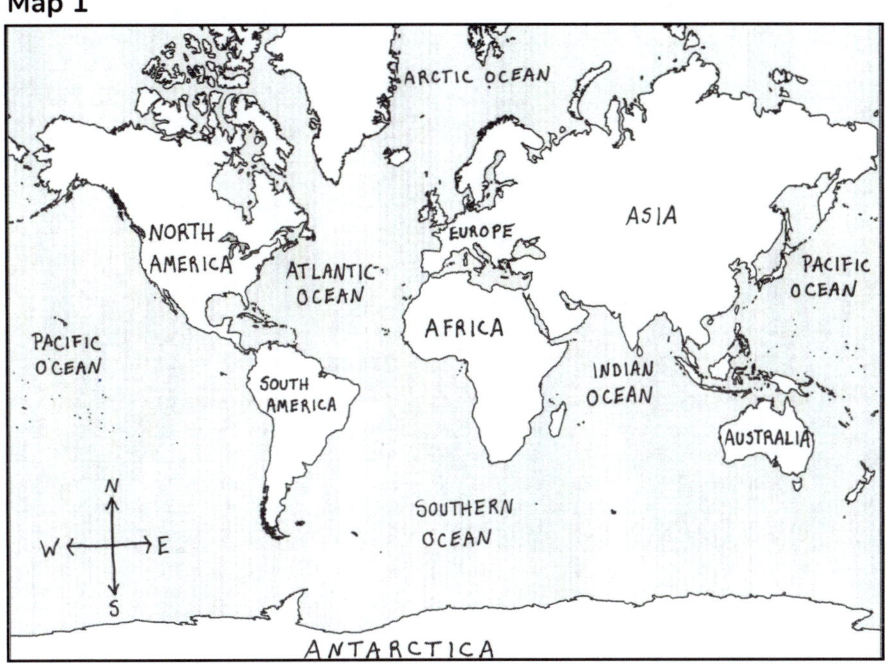

Map 2 (Key is for mapwork completed in Unit 2 and in Unit 6)

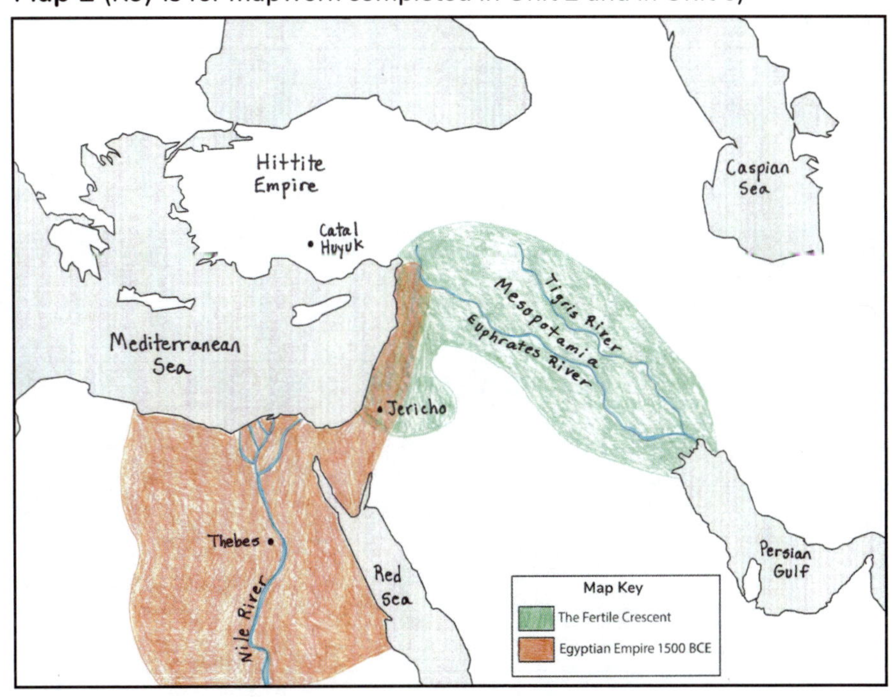

Map 3

COLOMBIA
ECUADOR
PERU
Amazon River
BRAZIL
PACIFIC OCEAN
BOLIVIA
CHILE
ARGENTINA
Map Key
Ancient Nazca Civilization
Andes Mountains

Map 4

Carthage
Mediterranean Sea
Sidon
Tyre
Jerusalem
Mesopotamia
EGYPT
Nile River

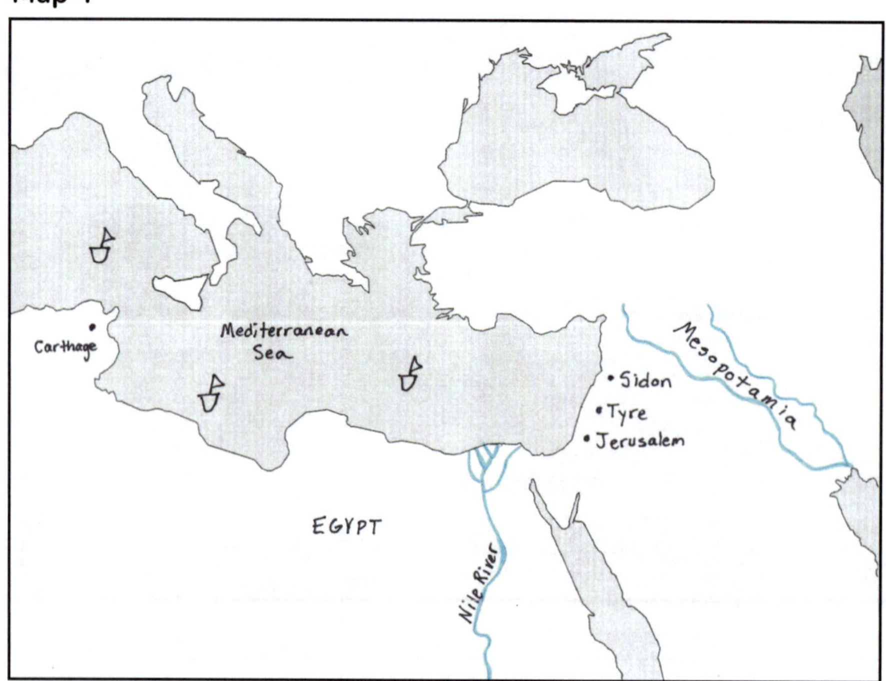

Map 5

Mount Olympus
GREECE
Thebes
Athens
Corinth
Sparta
Messene
Mediterranean Sea
CRETE

Map 6

Black Sea
Caspian Sea
MACEDONIA
Gordium
GREECE
Guagamela
MESOPOTAMIA
Mediterranean Sea
Babylon
Persian Gulf
PERSIA
EGYPT
Red Sea
Nile River
INDIA
Arabian Sea
Map Key
Empire of Alexander the Great

Pandia PRESS

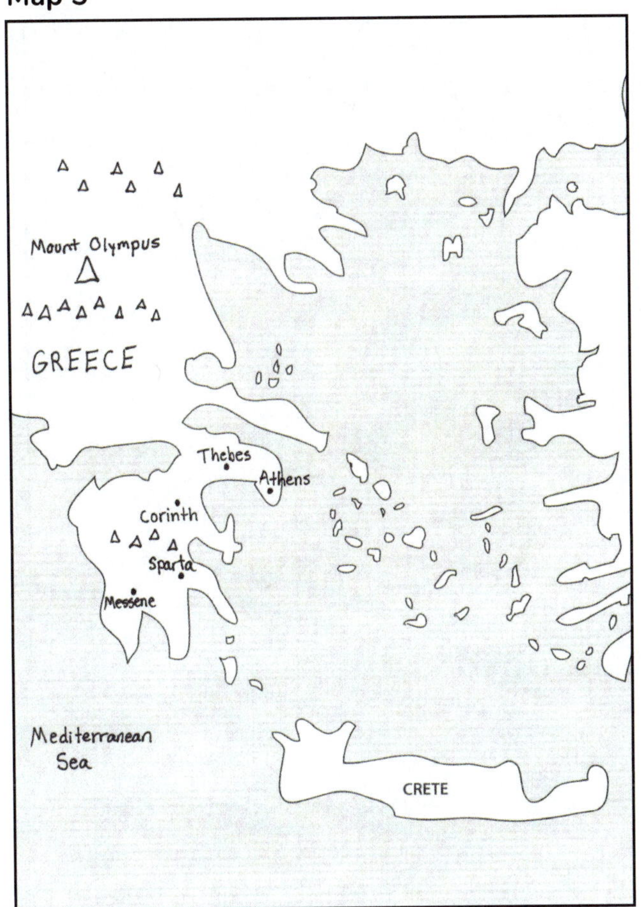

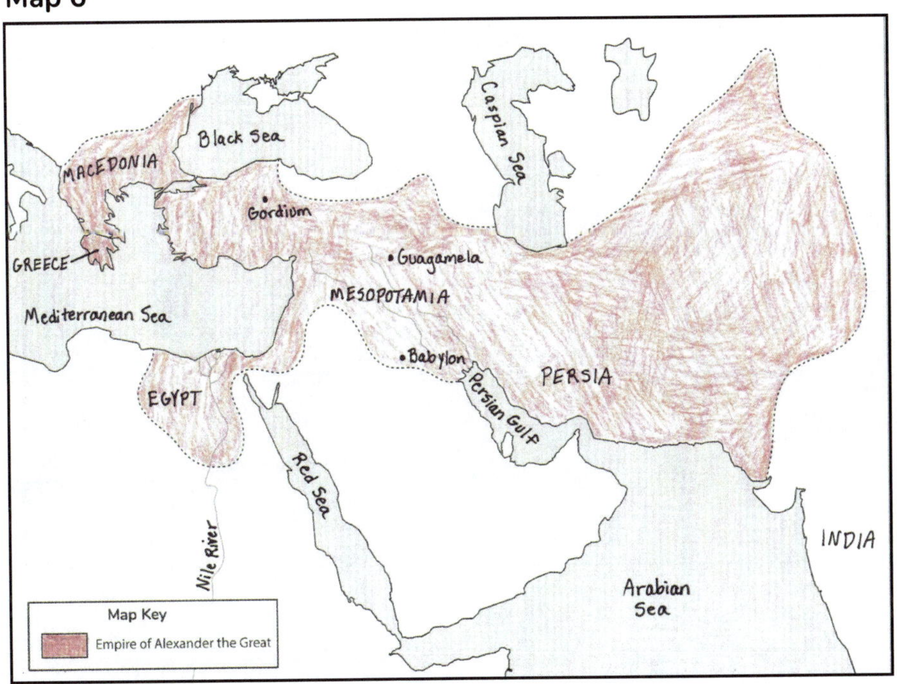

Map 7

PAKISTAN
Indus River
Harappa
Mohenjo-Daro
Himalayas
Ganges River
INDIA
Arabian Sea
Bay of Bengal
INDIAN OCEAN

Map 8

Alps
GAUL
Rubicon River
Tiber River
Rome
ITALY
SPAIN
SICILY
GREECE
Carthage
Mediterranean Sea
CRETE

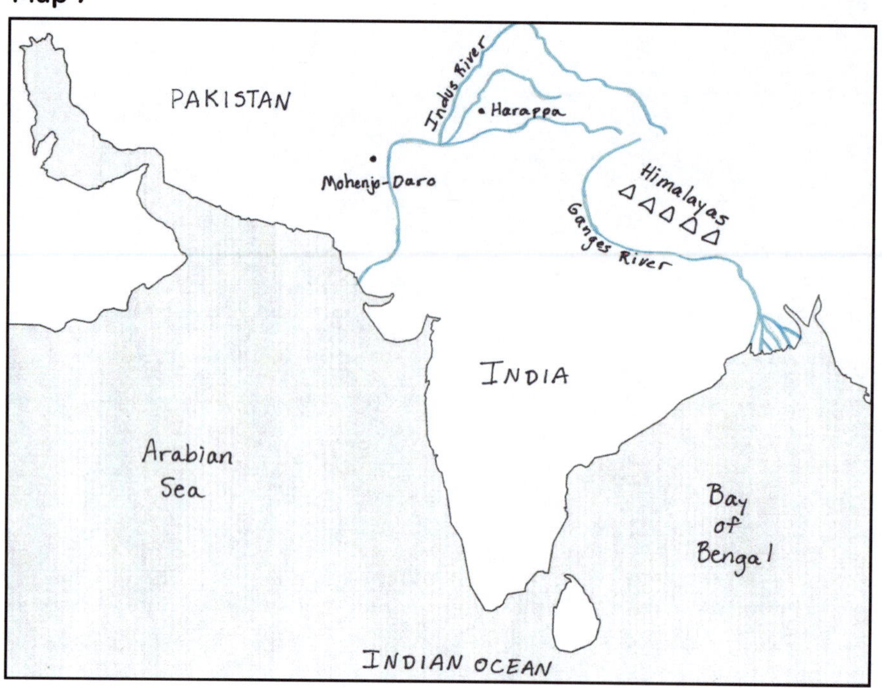

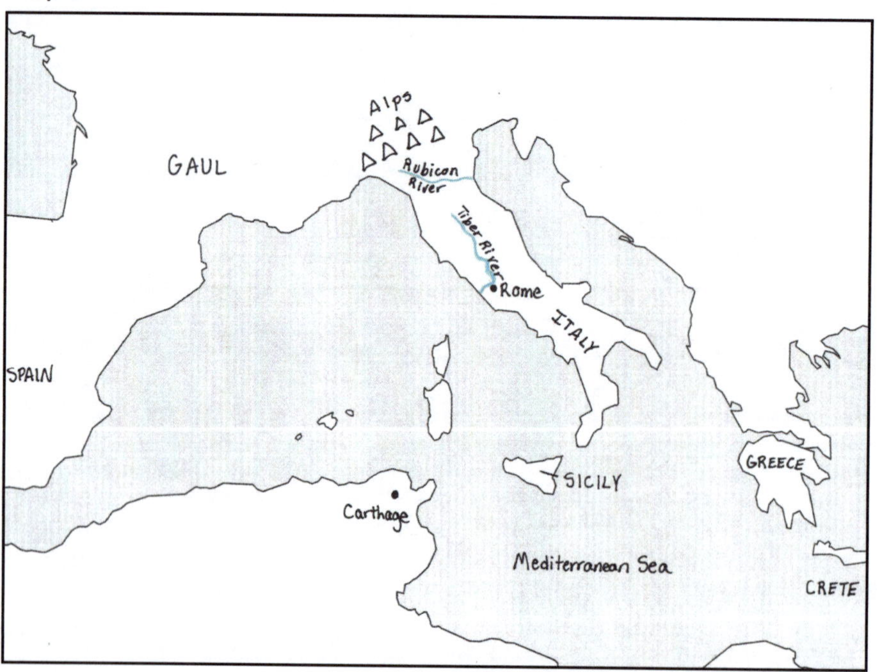

Map 9

Map Key
Western Roman Empire
Eastern Roman Empire
ENGLAND
ATLANTIC
OCEAN
FRANCE
Danube River
SPAIN
ITALY
Rome
BULGARIA
Black Sea
Byzantium
(Constantinople)
TURKEY
GREECE
MOROCCO
ALGERIA
Mediterranean Sea

Map 10

Map Key
Kush
Aksum
Mediterranean Sea
EGYPT
Sahara
Desert
Nile River
NUBIA
Napata
KUSH
Meroe
Red Sea
ARABIA
Adulis
AKSUM
INDIAN
OCEAN

Pandia PRESS

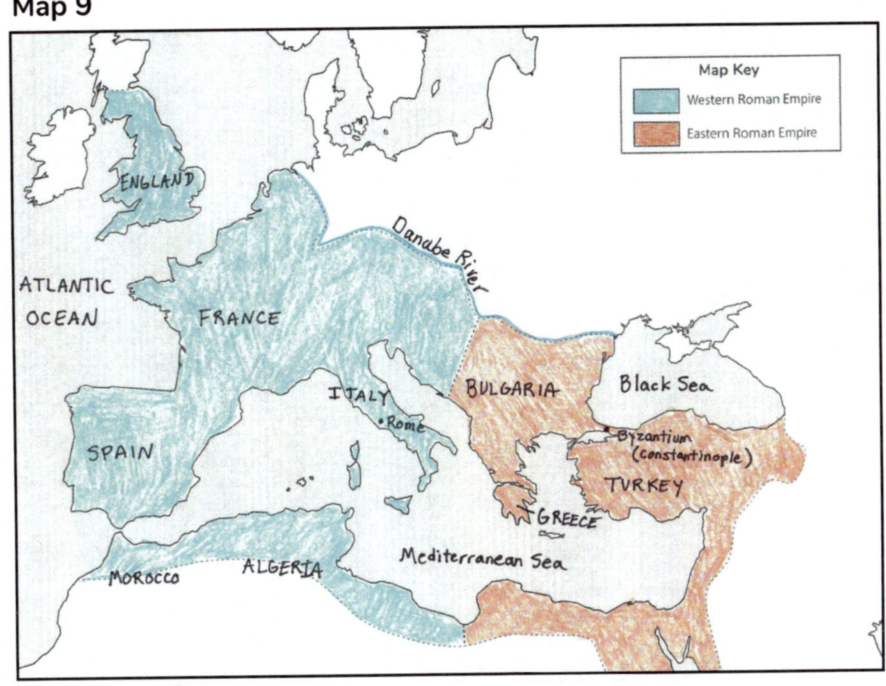

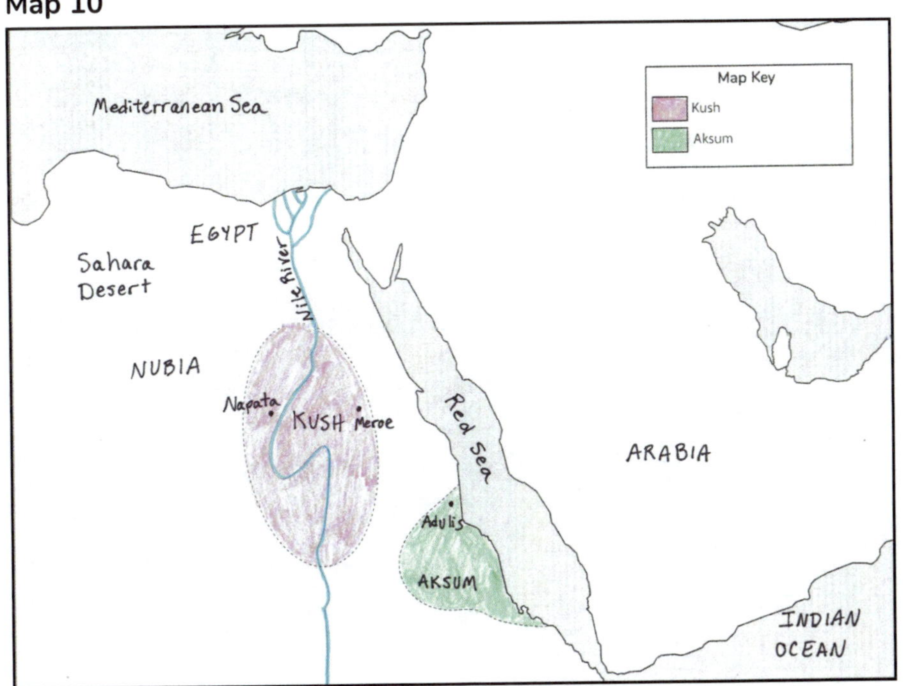

Map 11

Mediterranean Sea
Mesopotamia
Himalayas
Yellow River
CHINA
Yangtze River
PERSIA
EGYPT
ARABIA
INDIA
PACIFIC OCEAN
INDIAN OCEAN

Map 12

Kingdom of the Ostrogoths
ATLANTIC OCEAN
Kingdom of the Visigoths
ITALY
Rome
Black Sea
Constantinople
GREECE
Carthage
Mediterranean Sea
Kingdom of the Vanals
Jerusalem
Map Key
Byzantine Empire under Justinian
AFRICA
EGYPT
ARABIA

Pandia PRESS

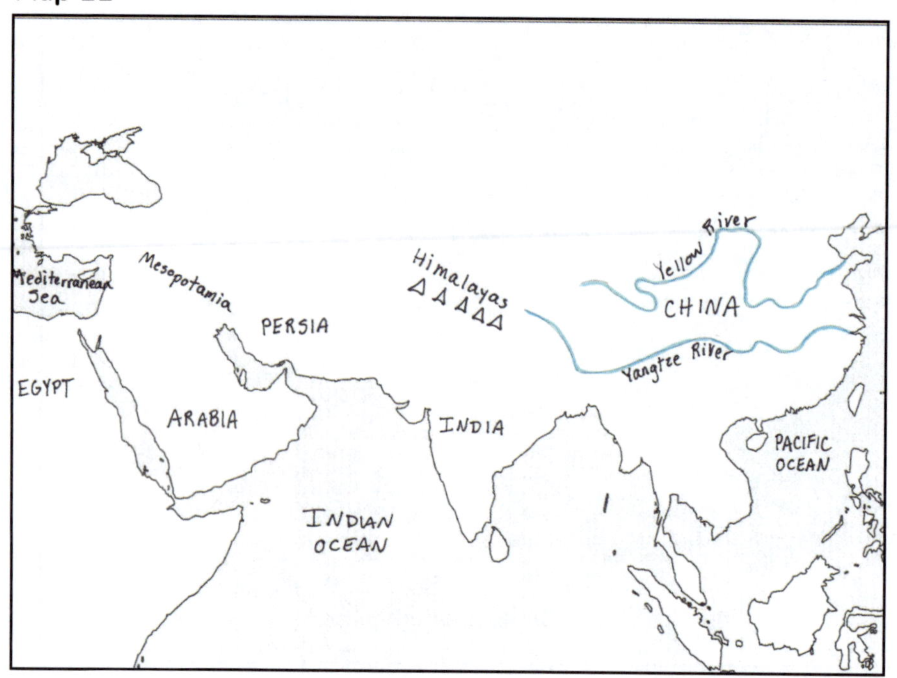

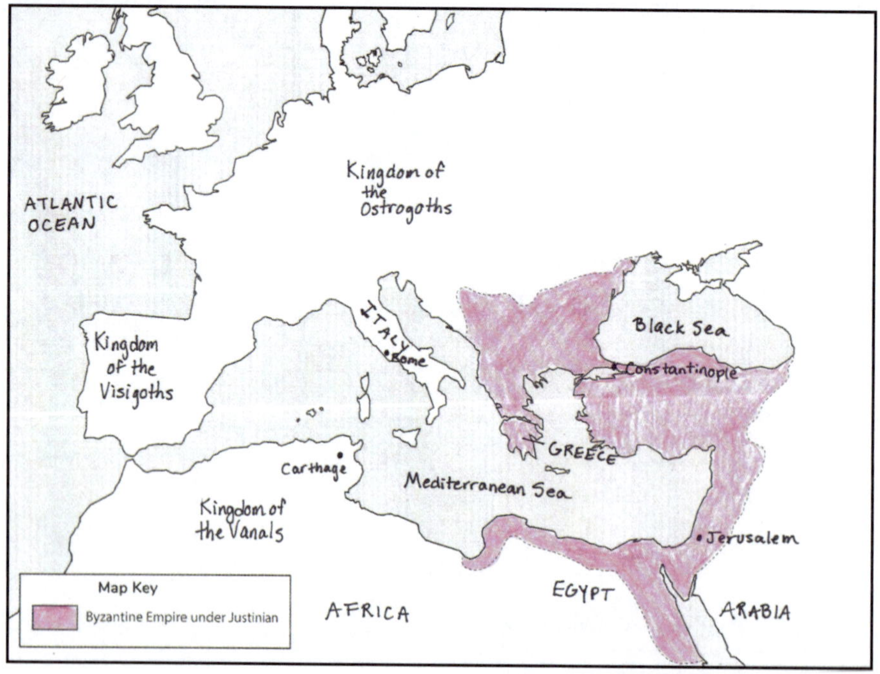

Map 13

SPAIN
Strait of Gibraltar
Constantinople
Mediterranean Sea
Damascus
Persian Gulf
Medina
Mecca
Red Sea
Adulis
Arabian Peninsula
Arabian Sea
Map Key
Islamic Empire at its greatest

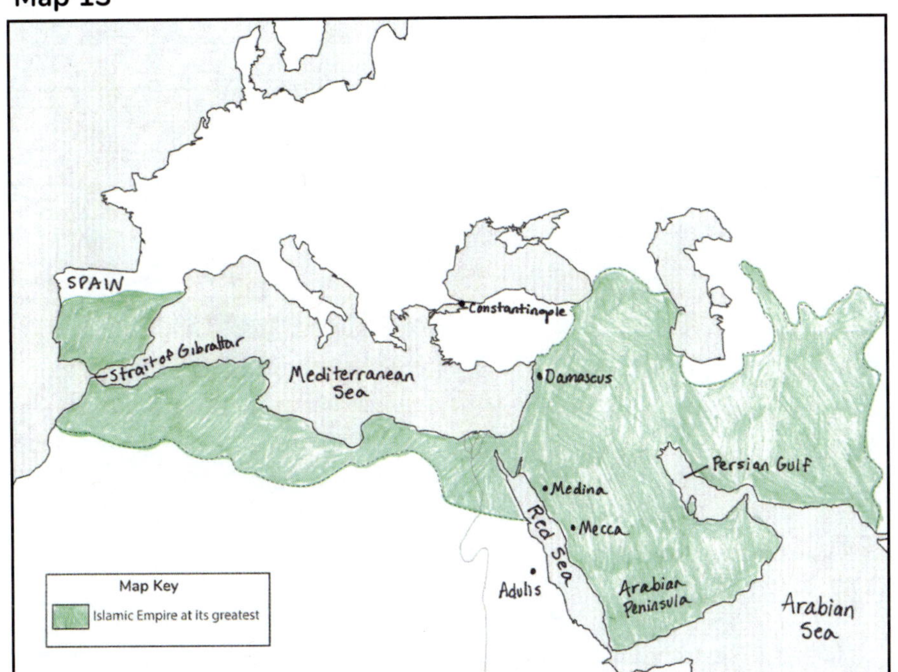

APPENDIX B: LITERATURE LIST

Title and Author	Unit	✓
Archaeologists Dig For Clues by Kate Duke	Intro	
Fossils Tell of Long Ago by Aliki	Intro	
Discovery in the Cave by Mark Dubowski	1	
The Secret Cave: Discovering Lascaux by Emily Arnold McCully	1	
The First Drawing by Mordicai Gerstein	1	
Stone Age Boy by Satoshi Kitamura	2	
Skara Brae: The Story of a Prehistoric Village by Olivier Dunrea	2	
Life in Ancient Mesopotamia by Shilpa Mehta-Jones	3	
DK Eyewitness Books: Ancient Civilizations by Joseph Fullman	3	
You Wouldn't Want to Live Without Writing! by Roger Canavan	3	
You Wouldn't Want to Be a Sumerian Slave! by Jacqueline Morley	4	
The Sumerians by Jane Shuter	4	
Gilgamesh the Hero by Geraldine McCaughrean	Hygge #1	
Gilgamesh the King by Ludmila Zeman	Hygge #1	
The Revenge of Ishtar by Ludmila Zeman	Hygge #1	
The Last Quest of Gilgamesh by Ludmila Zeman	Hygge #1	
Pharaoh's Boat by David L. Weitzman	5	
Mummies Made in Egypt by Aliki	5	
Pyramid, a PBS documentary film or book by David Macaulay	5	
Seeker of Knowledge: The Man Who Deciphered Egyptian Hieroglyphs by James Rumford	6	
Horrible Histories: The Awesome Egyptians by Terry Deary and Peter Hepplewhite	6	
DK Eyewitness Books: Ancient Egypt by George Hart	6	
The Shipwrecked Sailor: An Egyptian Tale with Hieroglyphs by Tamara Bower	6	
How the Amazon Queen Fought the Prince of Egypt by Tamara Bower	6	
Spotlight on Peru by Robin Johnson and Bobbie Kalman	7	
The Llama's Secret: A Peruvian Legend by Argentina Palacios	7	
Alpacas by Michelle Hasselius	7	
Popol Vuh: A Sacred Book of the Maya by Victor Montejo	8	
The Ancient Maya by Jackie Maloy	8	
Mesopotamia by Sunita Apte	9	

Title and Author	Unit	✓
The Usborne Encyclopedia of World Religions by Susan Meredith	12	
You Wouldn't Want to Be a Greek Athlete! by Michael Ford	13	
DK Eyewitness Books: Ancient Greece by Anne Pearson	13	
The Wanderings of Odysseus by Rosemary Sutcliff	13	
Black Ships Before Troy by Rosemary Sutcliff	Hygge #2	
D'Aulaires' Book of Greek Myths by Ingri d'Aulaire and Edgar Parin d'Aulaire	Hygge #2	
Sports Heroes of Ancient Greece by Paul Mason	14	
The Spartan Hoplites by Louise Park and Timothy Love	14	
The Librarian who Measured the Earth by Kathryn Lasky	15	
Everyday Life in Ancient Greece by Anne Pearson	15	
Alexander the Great by Demi	16	
Building History: Indus Valley City by Gillian Clements	17	
The Indus Valley by Jane Shuter	17	
The Elephant's Friend and Other Tales from Ancient India by Marcia Williams	18	
Ganesha's Sweet Tooth by Sanjay Patel and Emily Haynes	18	
Ramayana: Divine Loophole by Sanjay Patel	Hygge #3	
DK Eyewitness Books: Ancient Rome by Simon James	19	
Cleopatra by Diane Stanley	20	
Pompeii…Buried Alive! by Edith Kunhardt	20	
City: A Story of Roman Planning and Construction by David Macauley	20	
Roman Diary: The Journal of Iliona, Young Slave by Richard Platt	21	
African Beginnings by James Haskins	22	
Fa Mulan: The Story of a Woman Warrior by Robert D. San Souci	23	
Liu and the Bird: A Journey in Chinese Calligraphy by Catherine Louis	23	
Hidden Army: Clay Soldiers of Ancient China by Jane O'Connor	24	
The Emperor Who Built the Great Wall by Jillian Lin	24	
The Girl Who Became Emperor by Jillian Lin	24	
Chinese Children's Favorite Stories by Mingmei Yip	Hygge #4	
Stories of the Chinese Zodiac series by Li Jian	Hygge #4	
The Silk Route: 7,000 Miles of History by John S. Major	25	
1001 Inventions & Awesome Facts from Muslim Civilization by National Geographic	26	

APPENDIX C: STUDENT PAGES

My Early Times History Notebook cover sheet

History Travel Log template* (2 pages)

History Travel Log Illustrations (26 illustrations)

Maps (13 maps)

Cuneiform Alphabet

Egyptian Hieroglyphs

Cartouche Template

Stirrup Pot (2 pages)

Nazca Line Condor

Mayan Animal Glyphs

Minoan Pottery (2 pages)

Polyphemus

Roman Numerals

*You will need 26 copies of the History Travel Log template for this curriculum.
Visit www.pandiapress.com/historytravellog for a free PDF of the travel log for printing.

My Early Times History Notebook

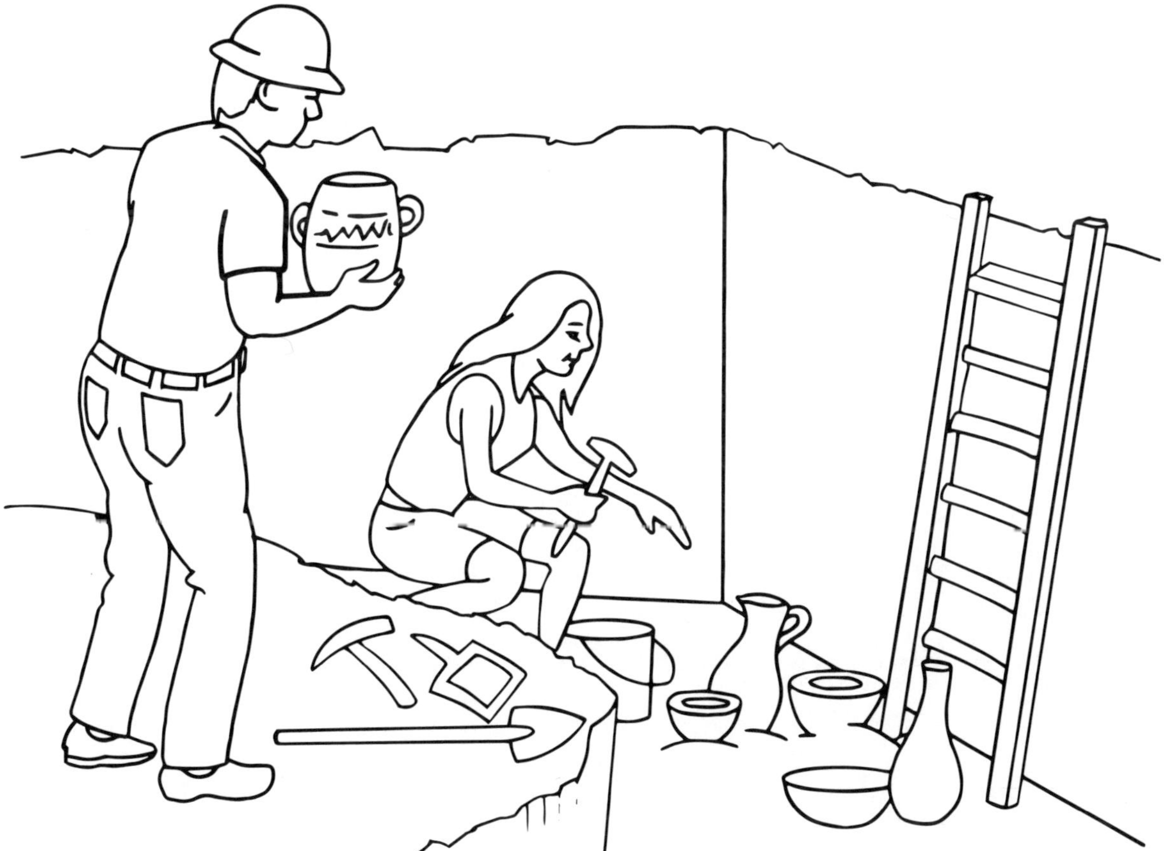

Pandia PRESS

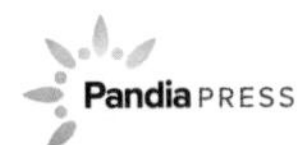

HISTORY TRAVEL LOG

I traveled to

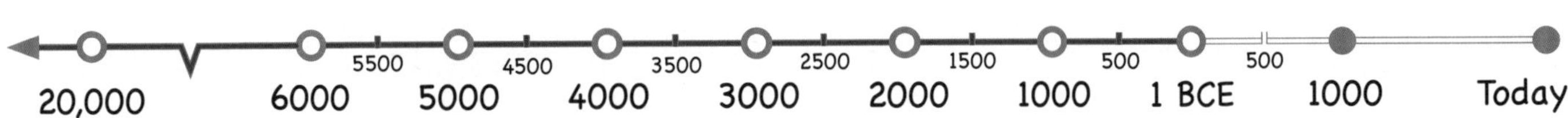

An illustration of what I found there . . .

During my travels to ______

I met . . .

I saw . . .

I learned . . .

History Travel Log Illustrations

The Knapper

The Stone Toolmakers

The Scribes

The First Author

The Chief Embalmer

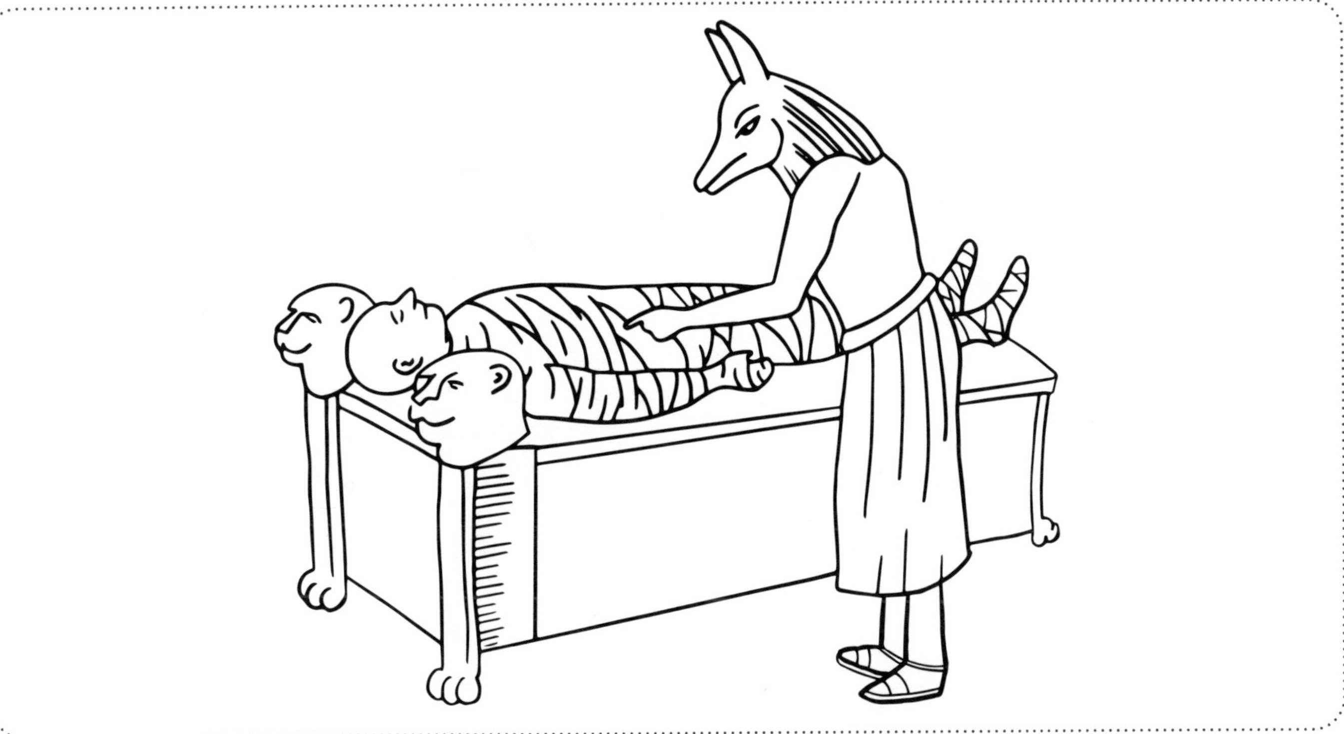

The Pharaoh

The Potter and the Weaver

The Hero Twins

The Babylonian Royal

The Ironworker

The Ally

The Sailor

The Legend

The Queen

The Citizen

The General

The City Planner

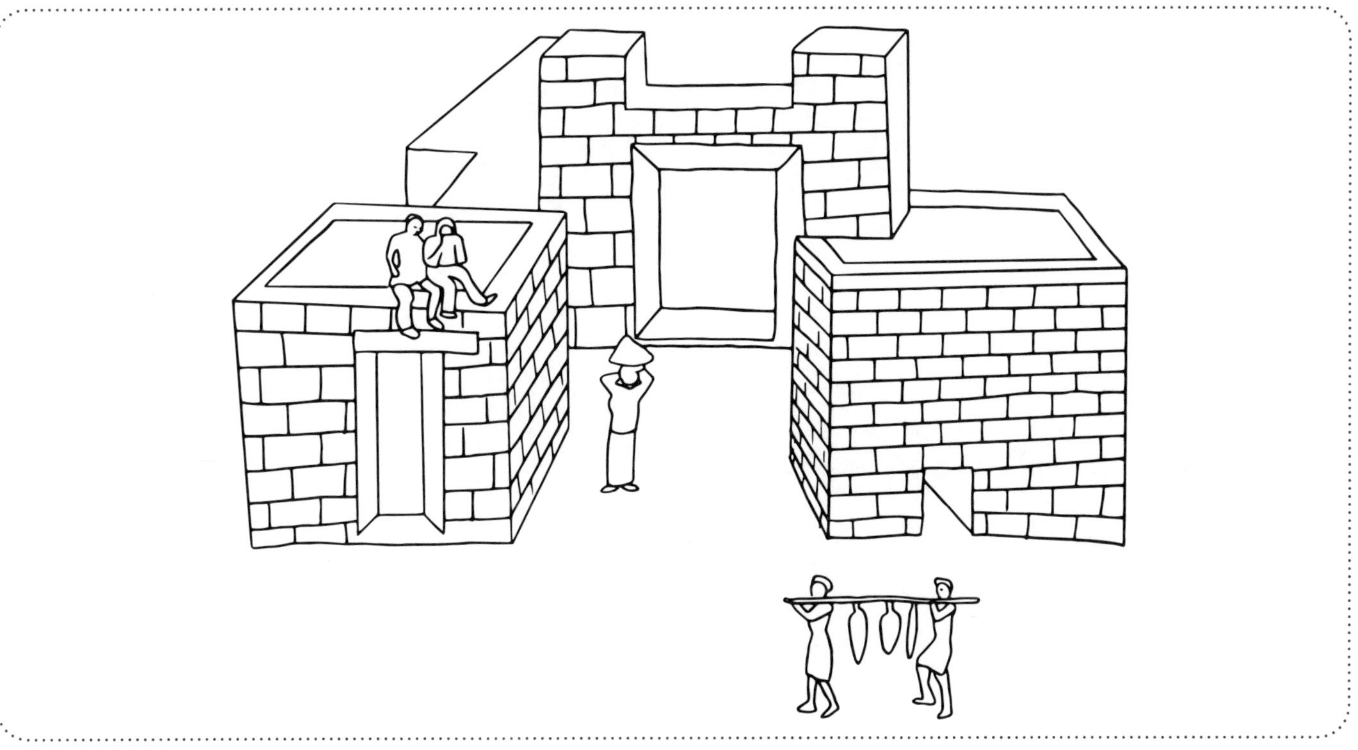

The Converted

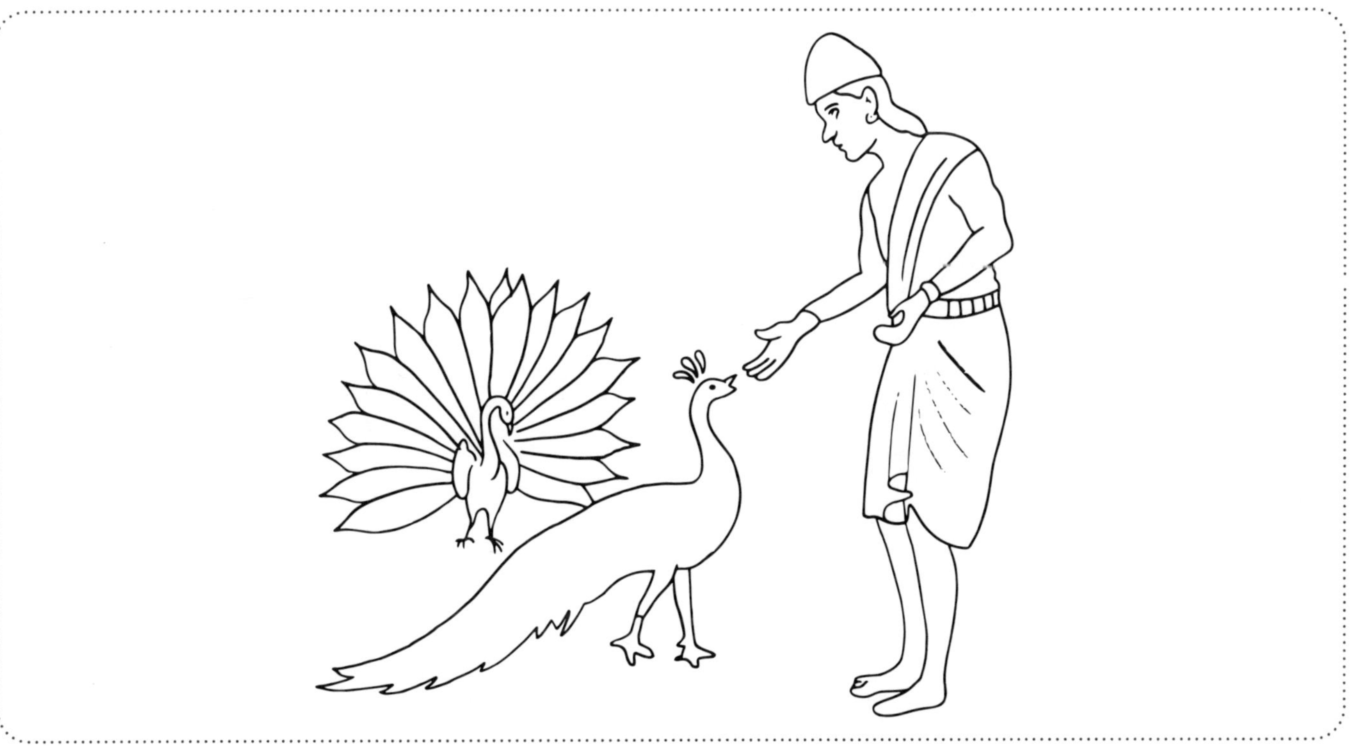

The Veteran

The Engineer

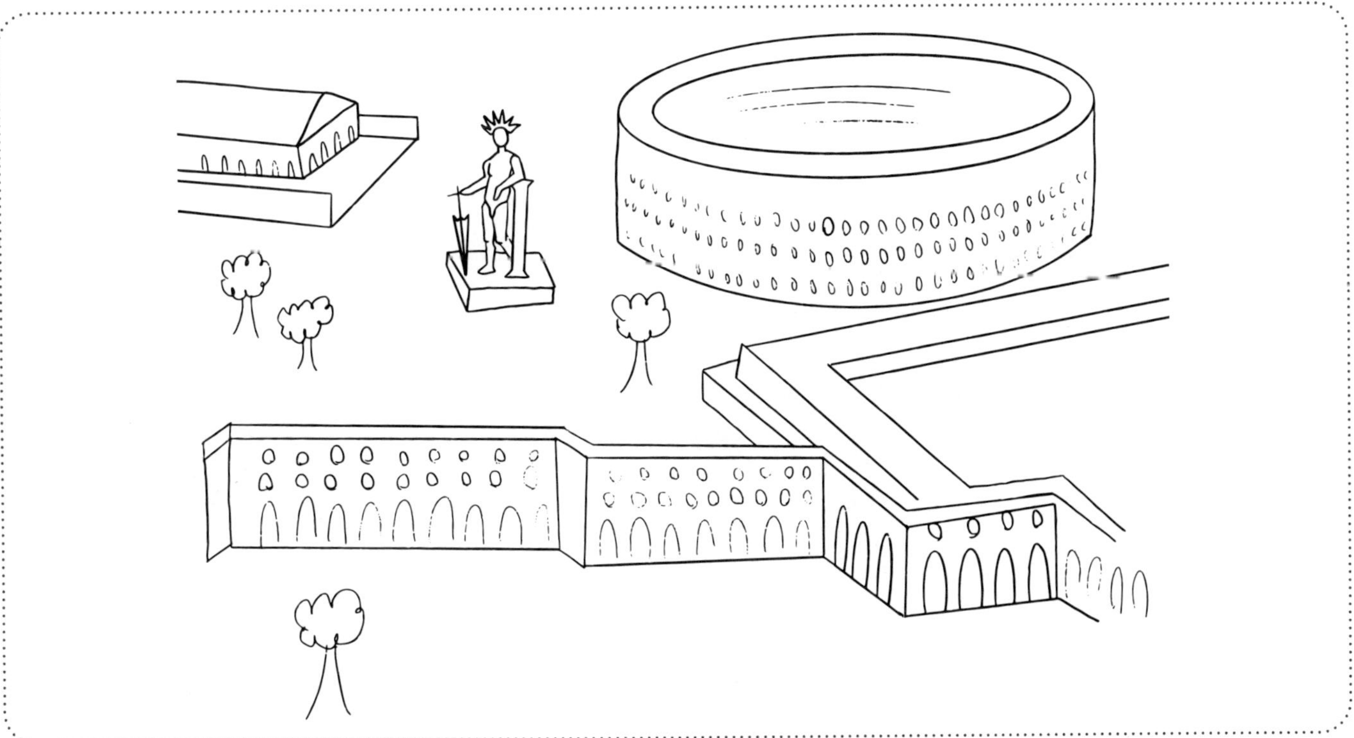

The Visigoth

The Merchants

The Silk Mother

The Scholar

The Circus Performer

The Caliph

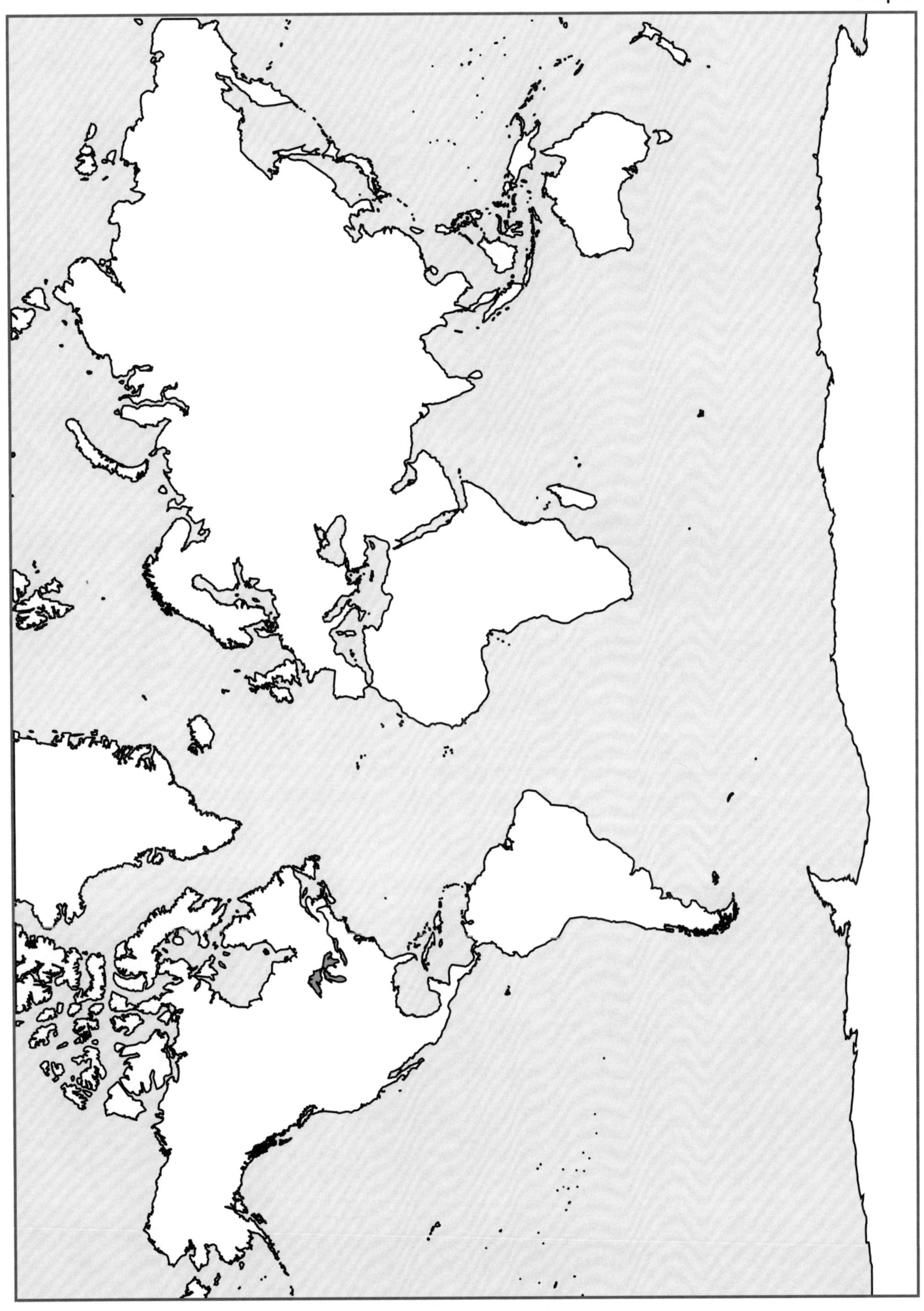

Map 2

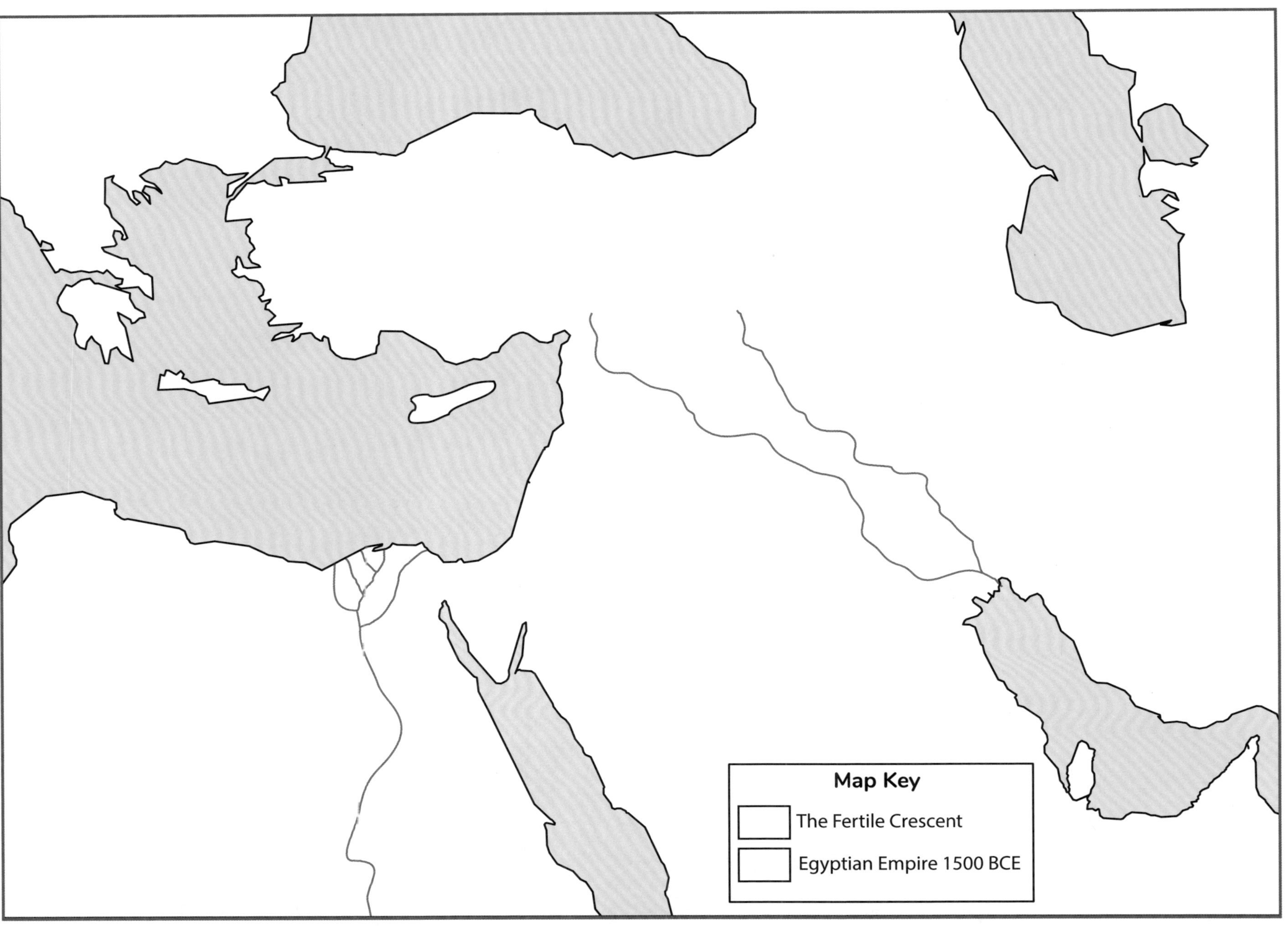

CHILE
ARGENTINA
Map Key
Ancient Nazca Civilization
Andes Mountains

Map 4

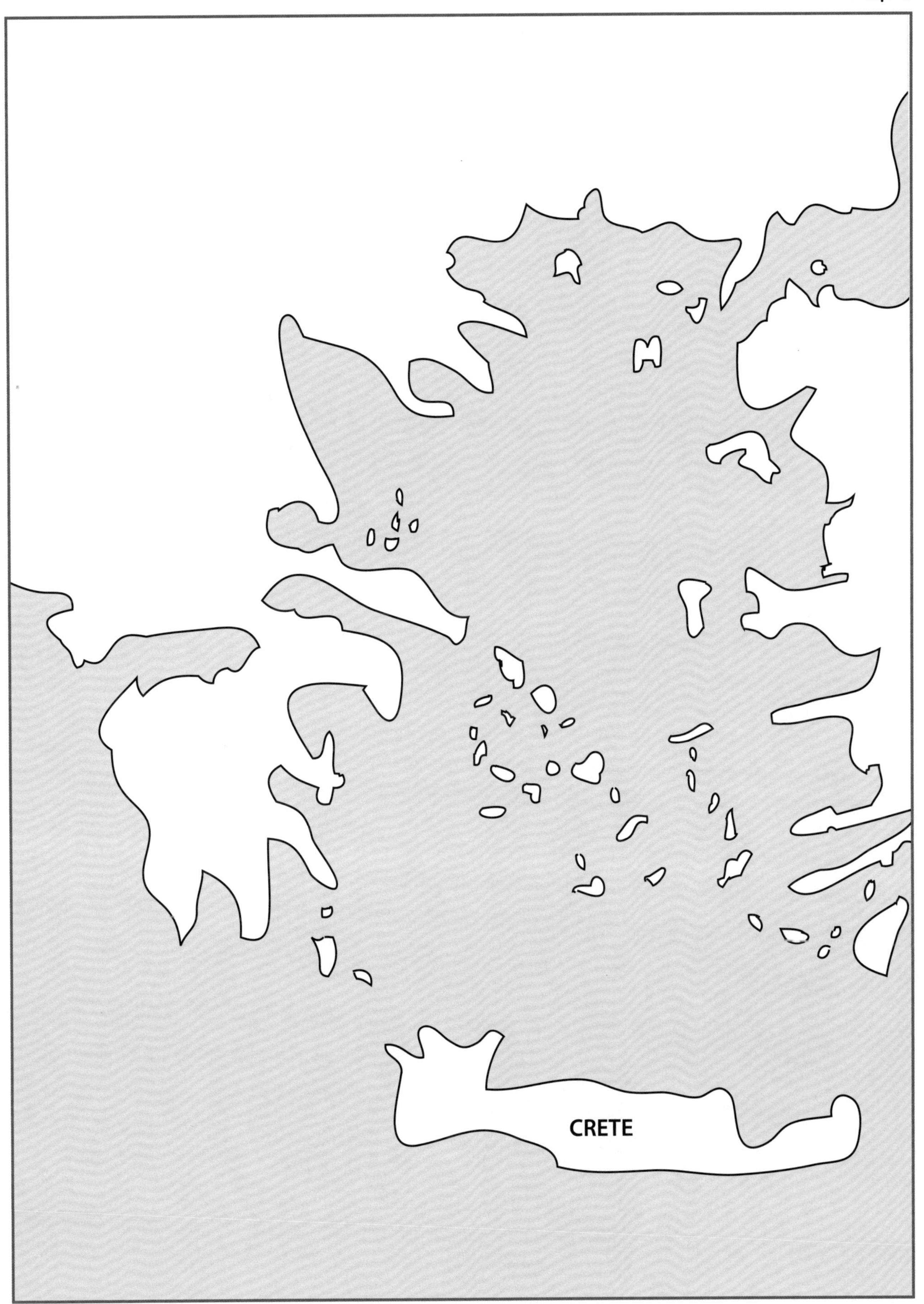
CRETE

Map 6

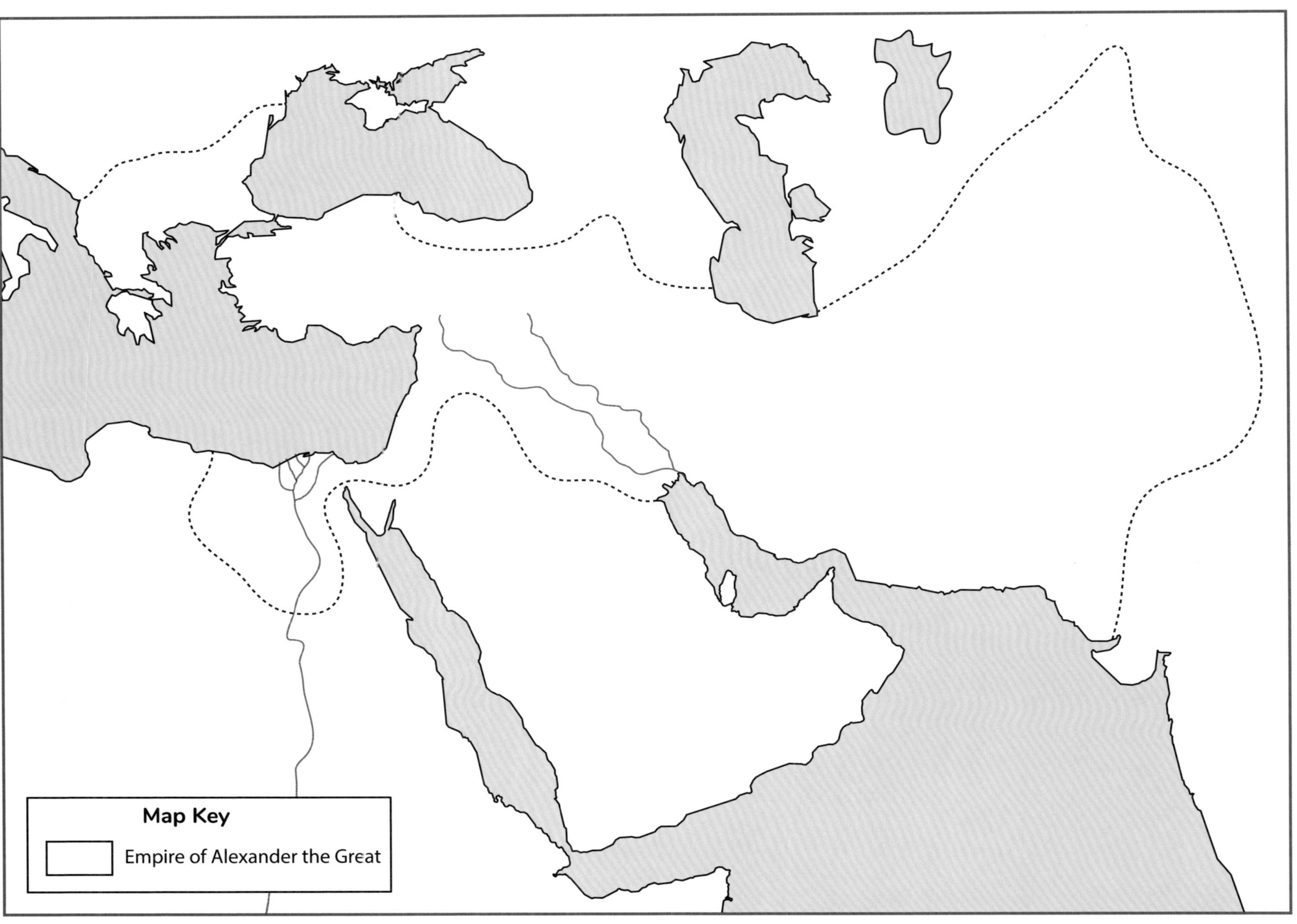

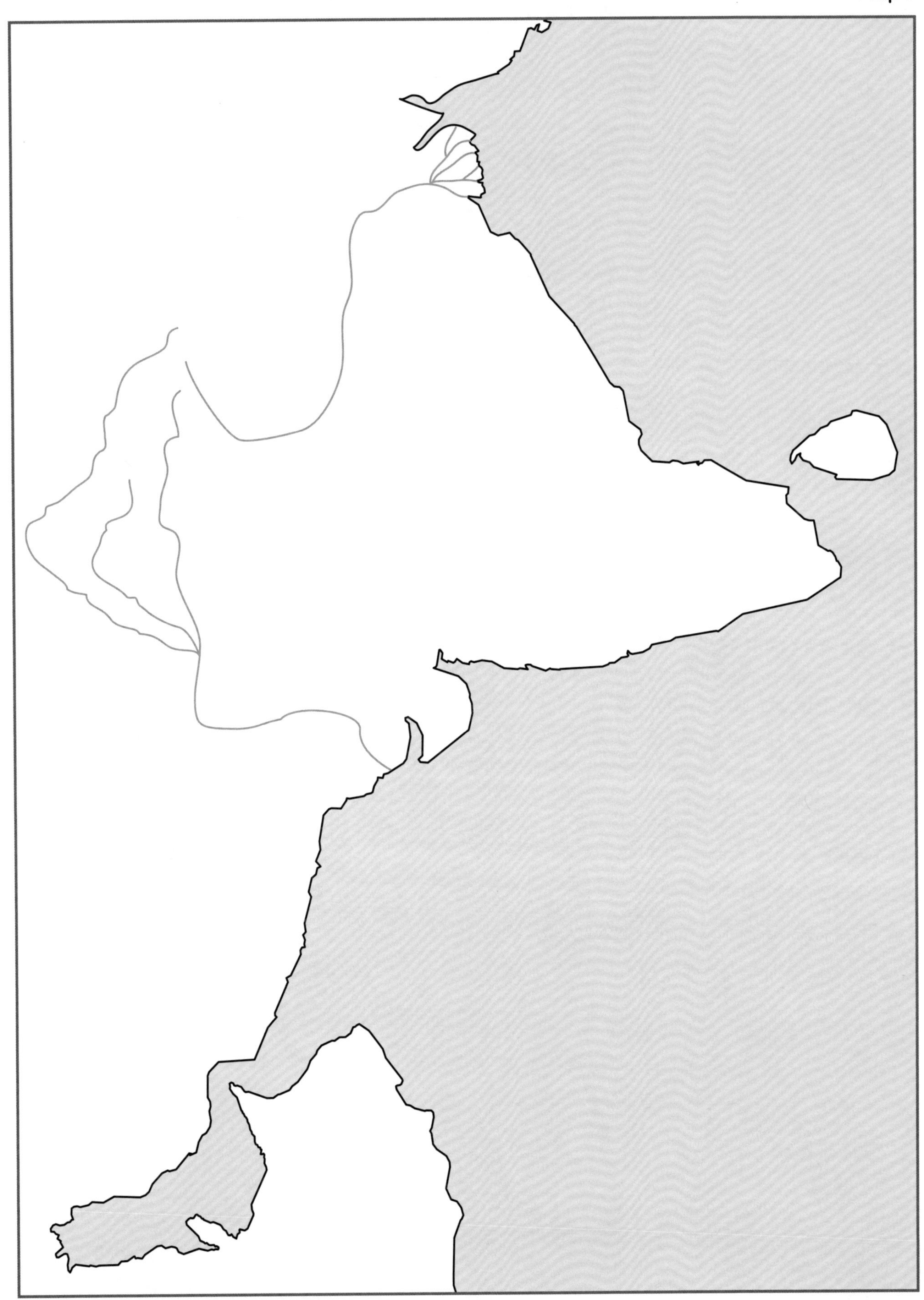

Map 8

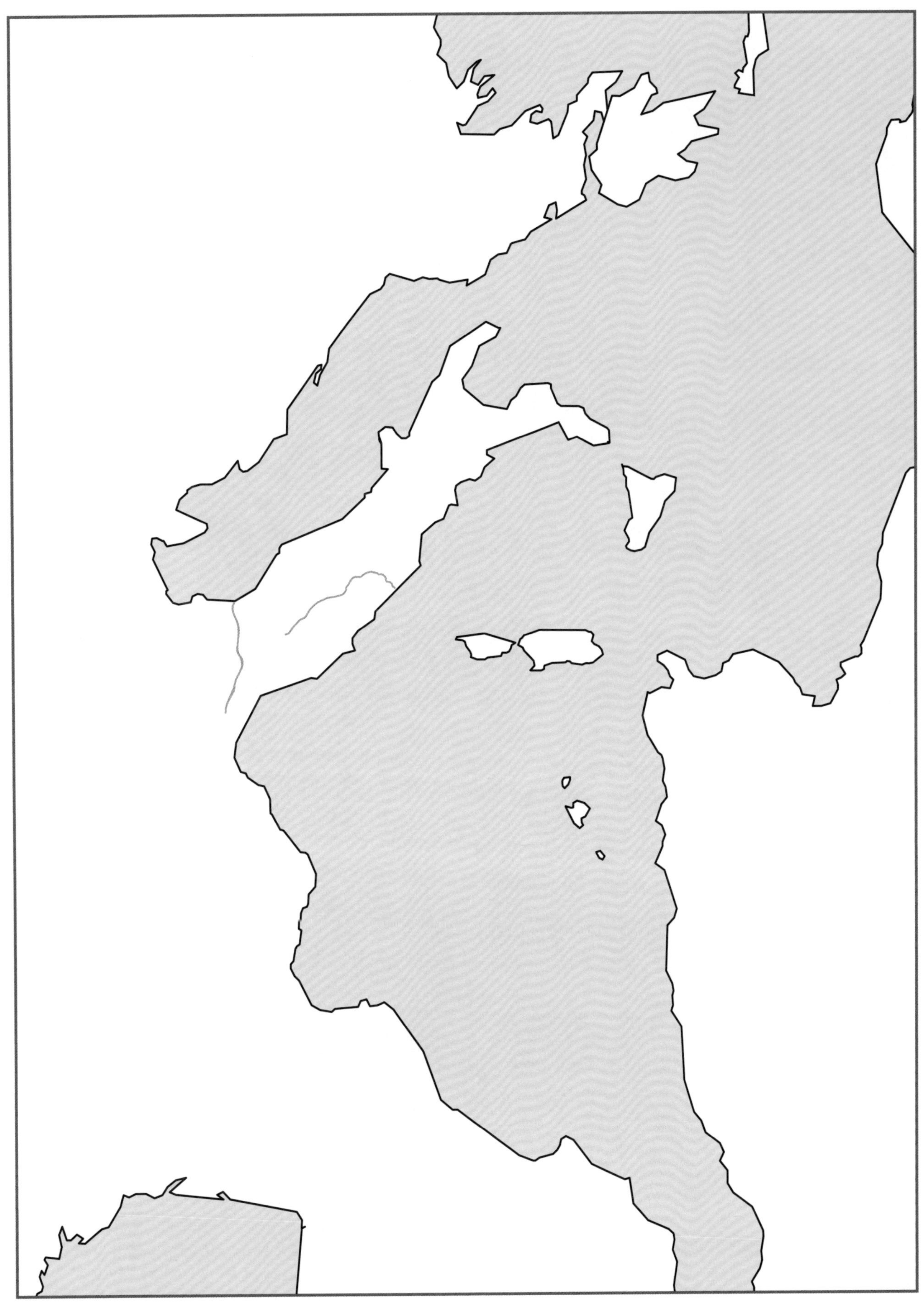

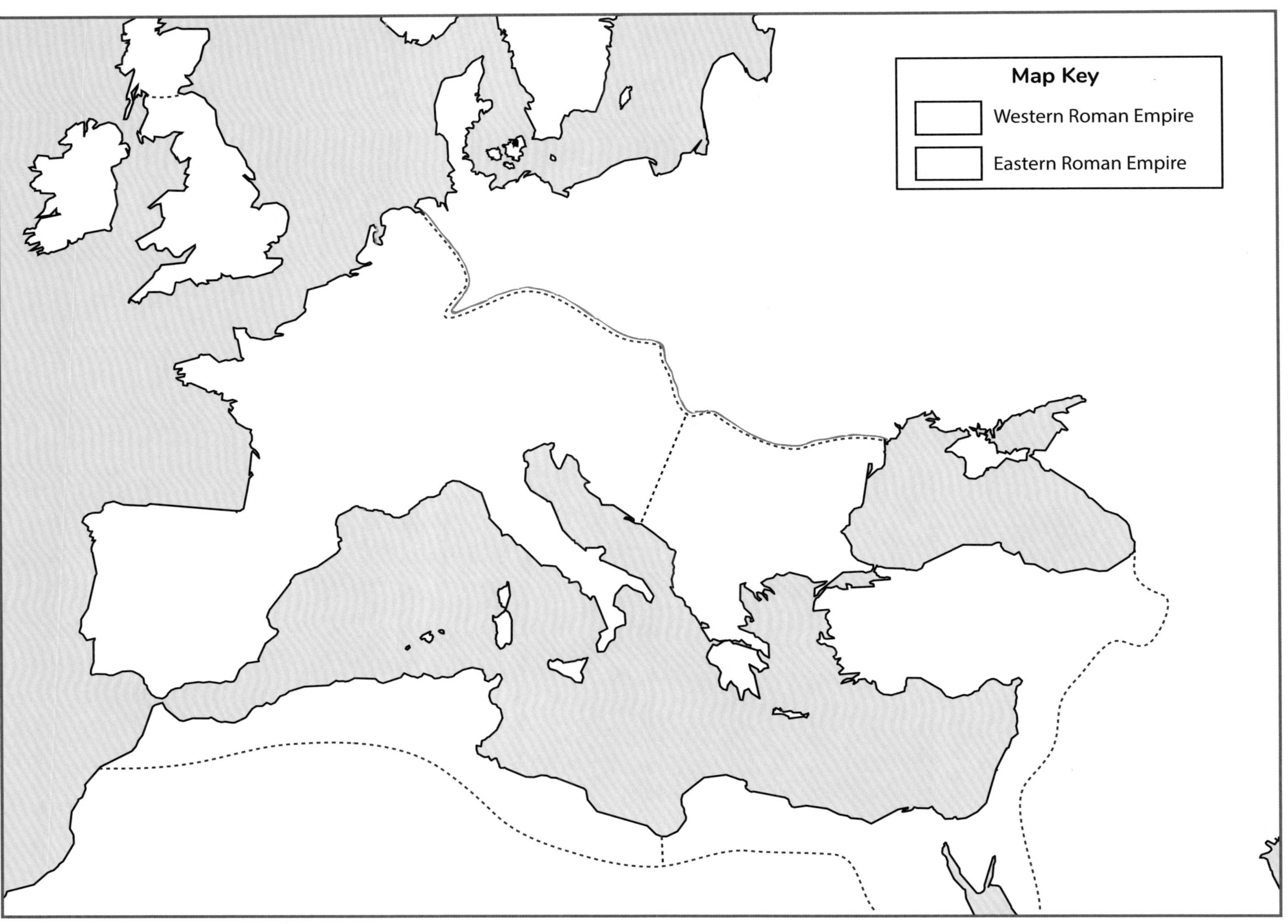
Map Key
Western Roman Empire
Eastern Roman Empire

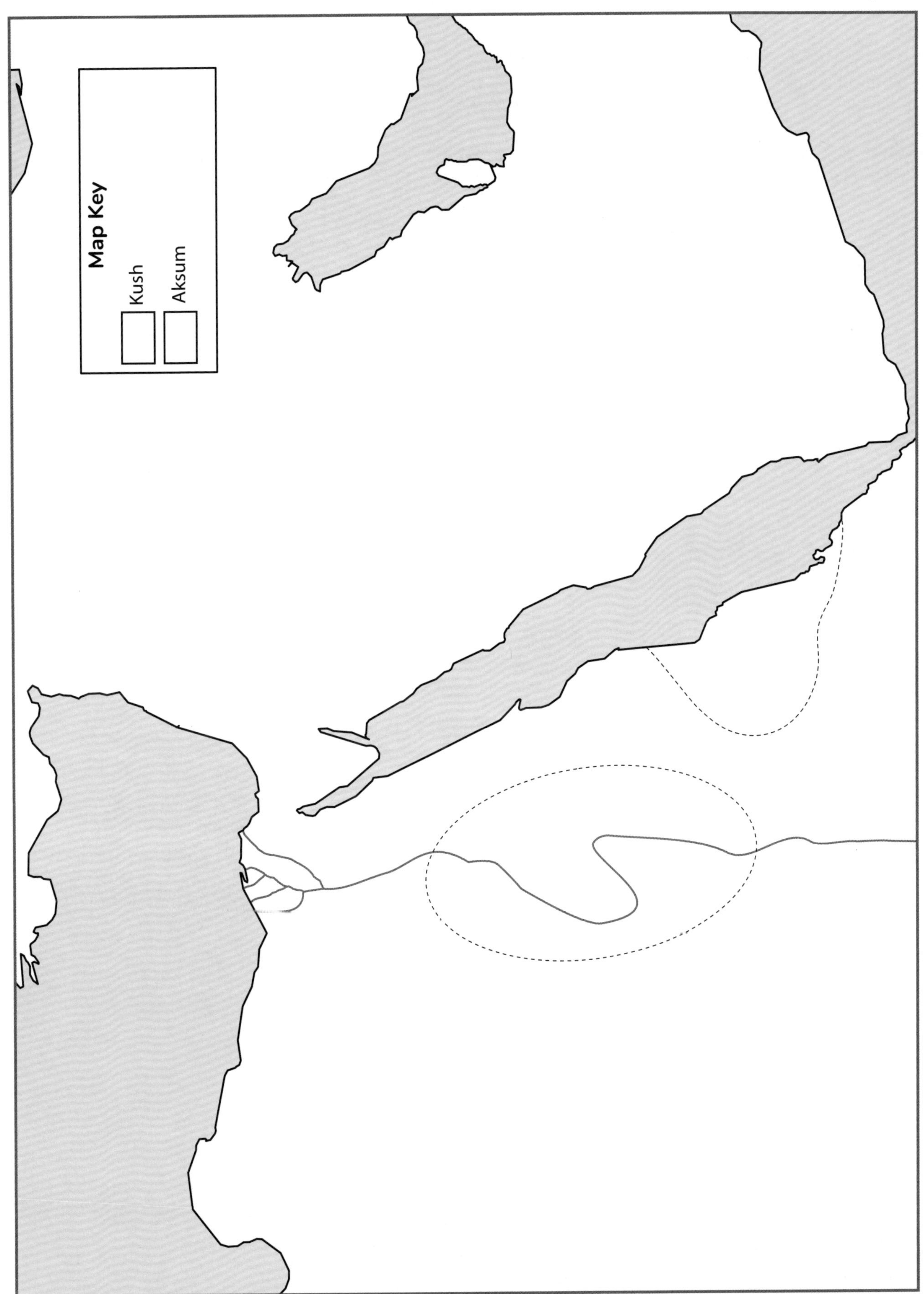
Map Key
Kush
Aksum

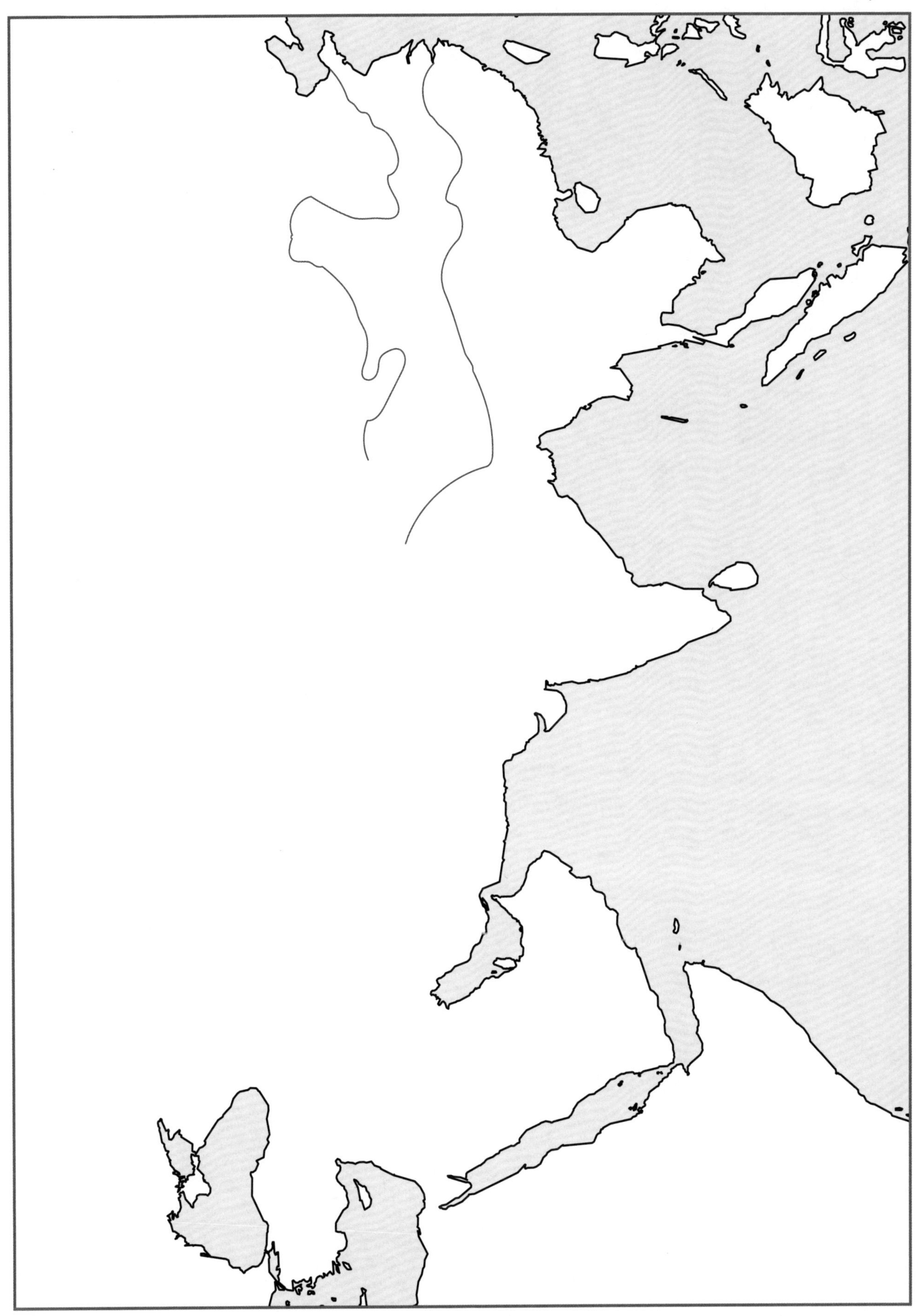

Map 12

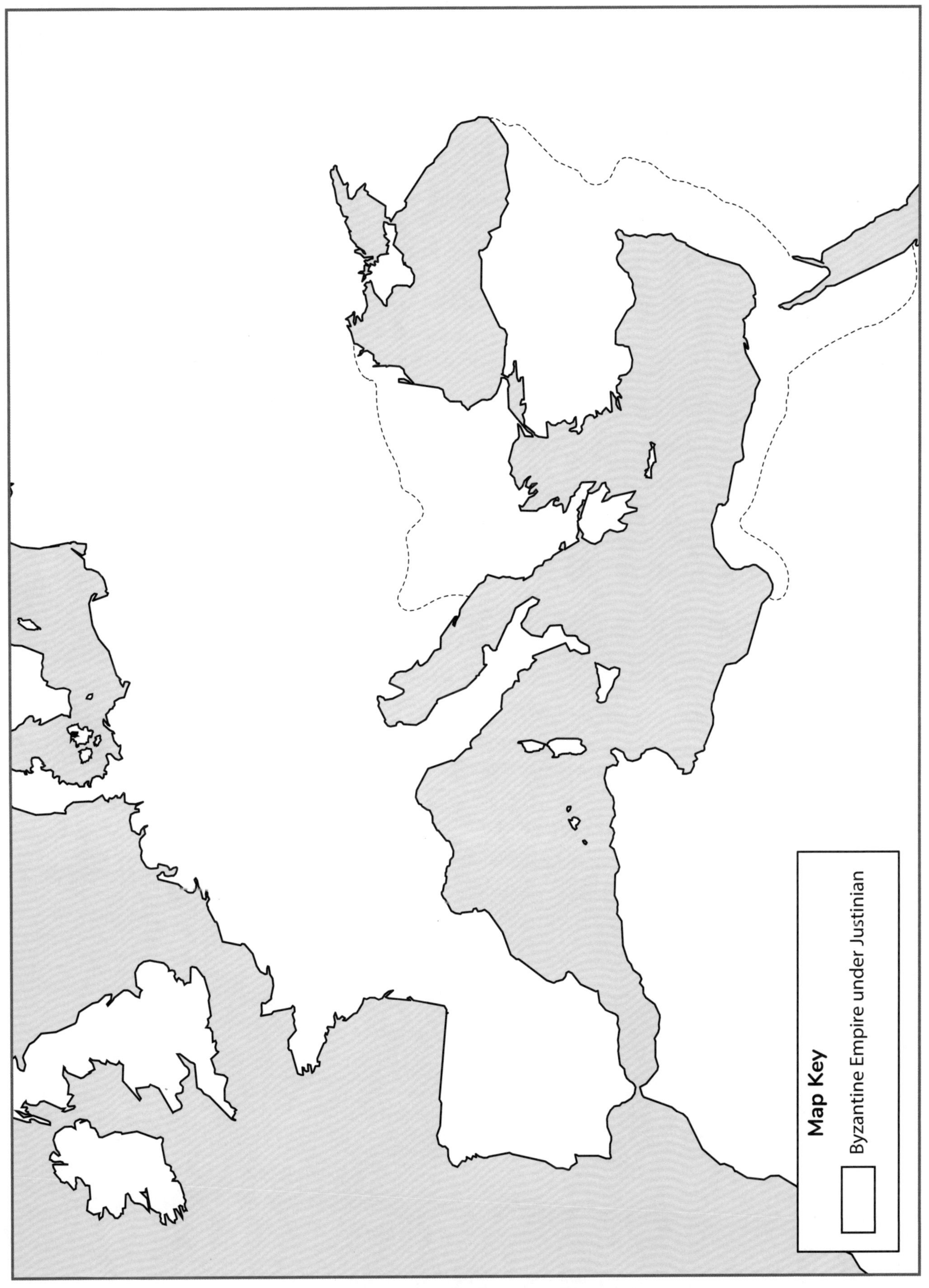

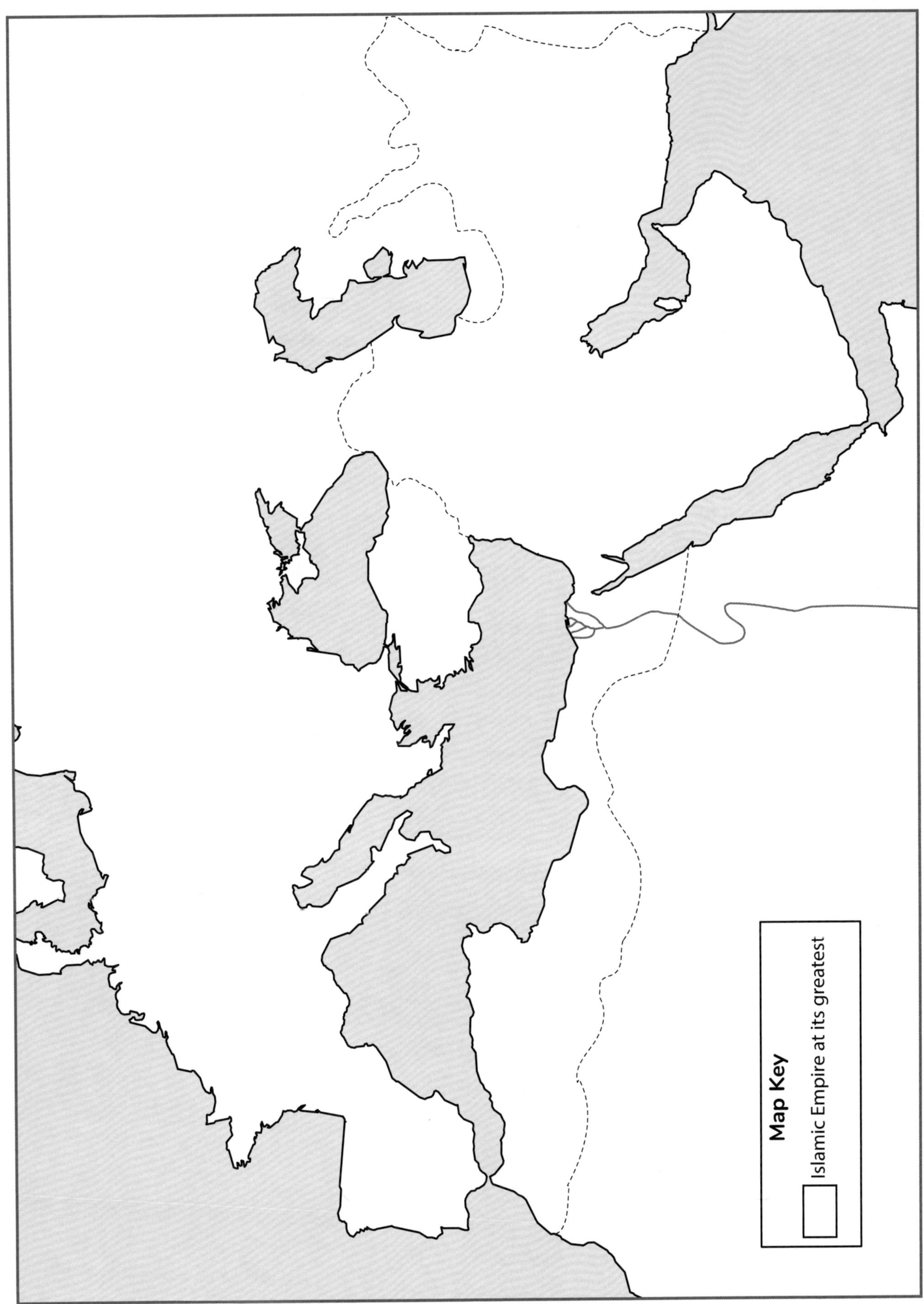
Map Key
Islamic Empire at its greatest

Cuneiform Alphabet

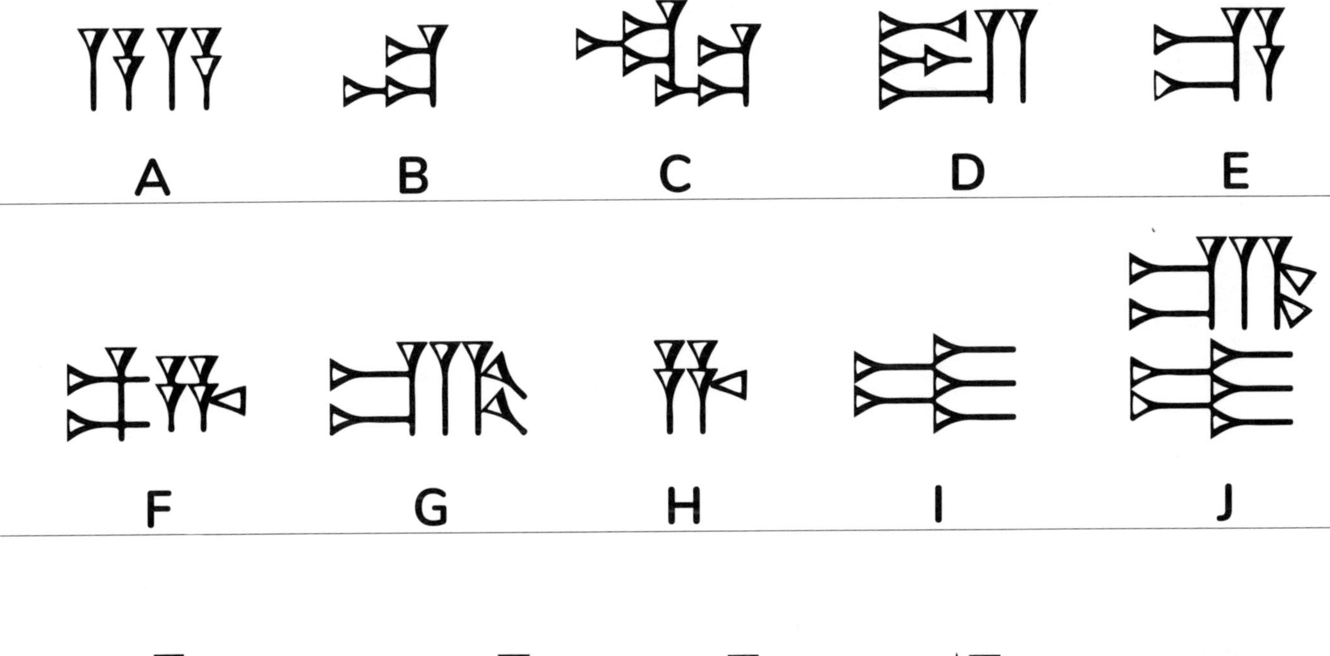

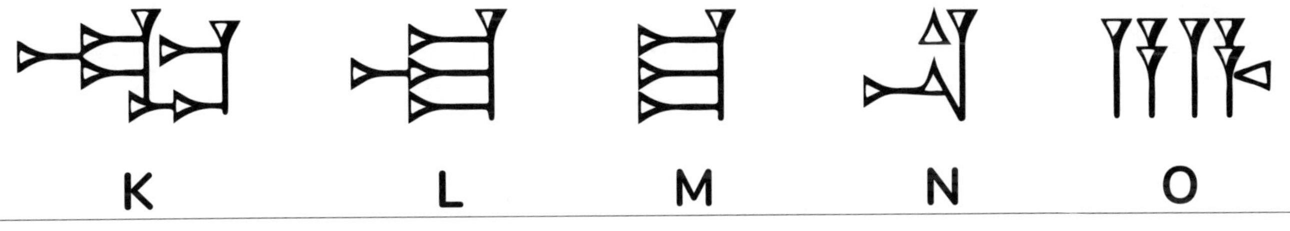

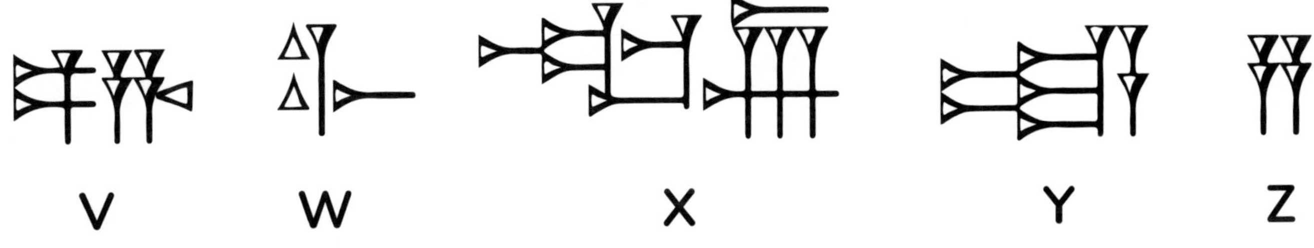

Egyptian Hieroglyphs

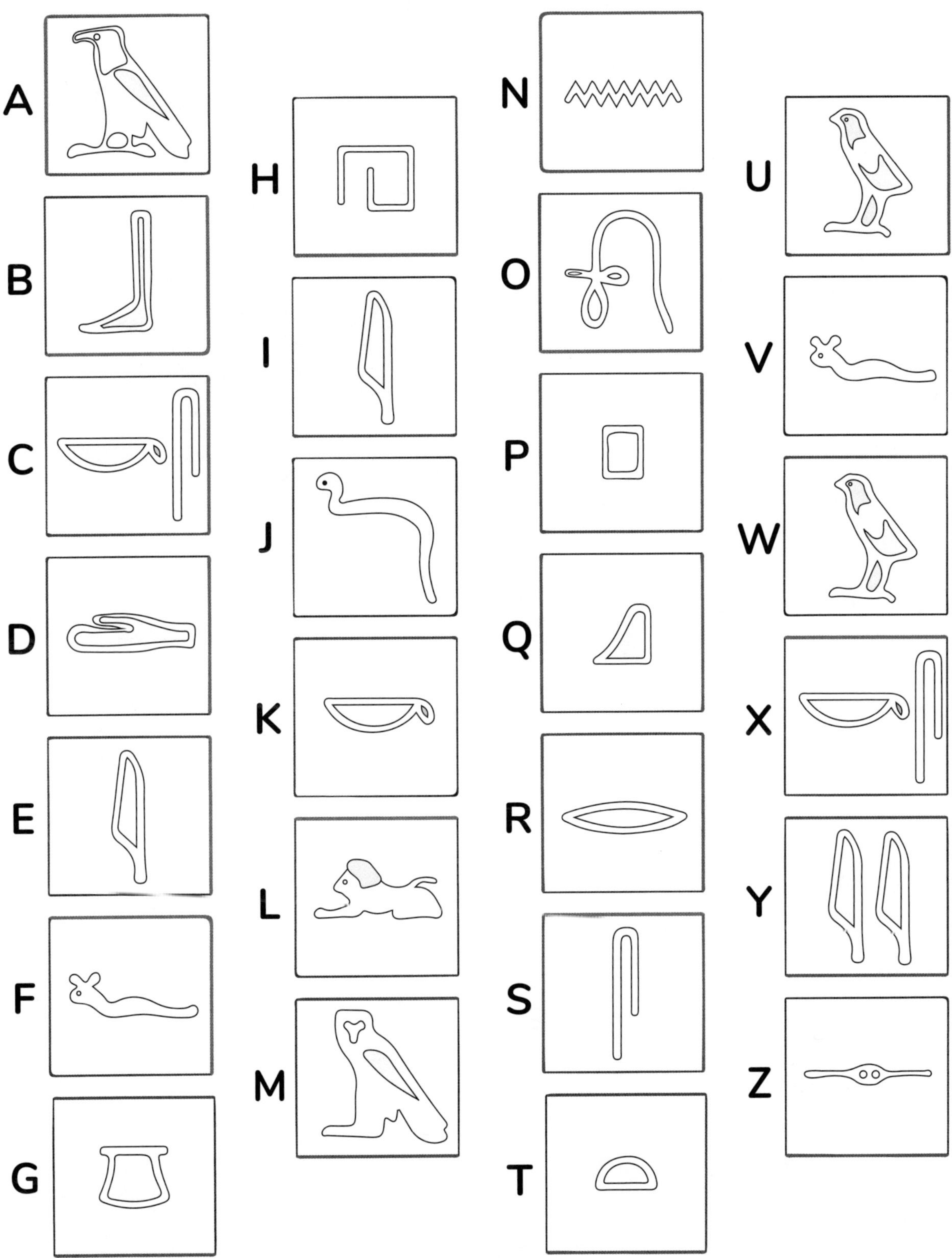

Cartouche Template

Stirrup Pot #1

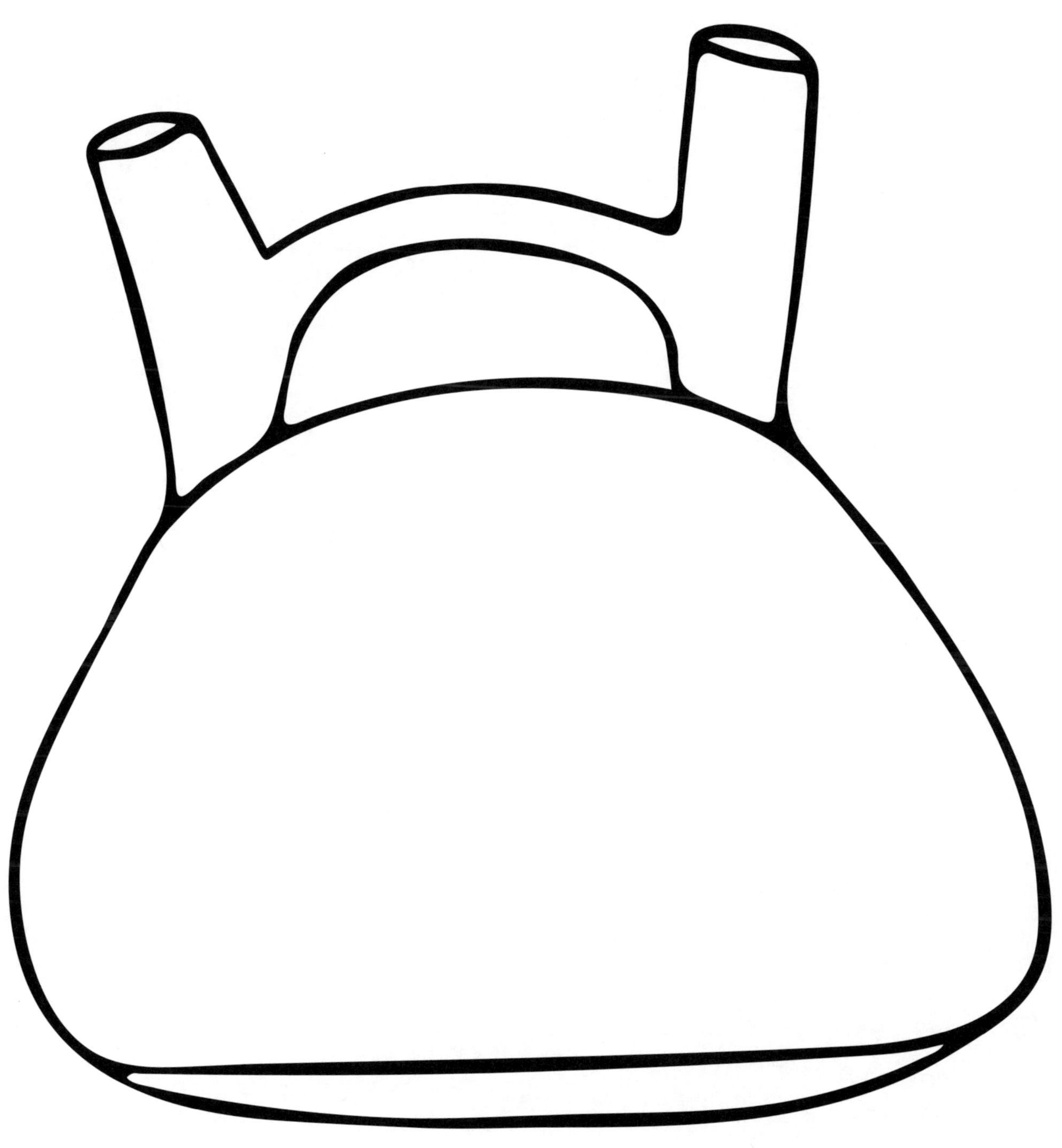

Stirrup Pot #2

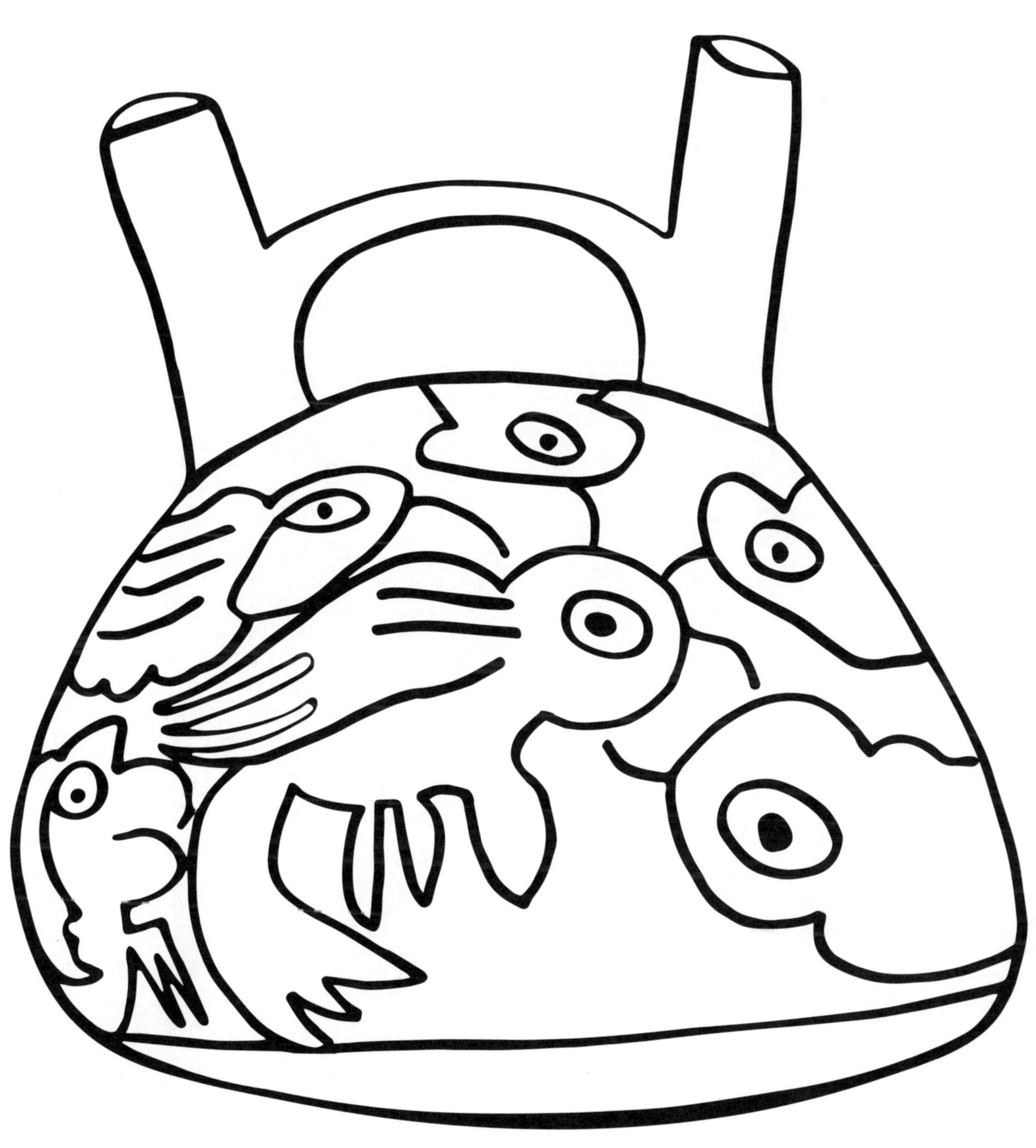

Condor Nazca Line

Mayan Animal Glyphs

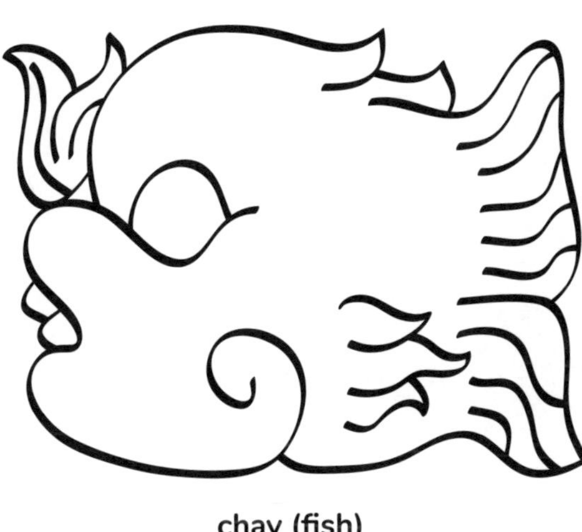

chay (fish)

suutz (bat)

ahk (turtle)

tzul (dog)

ahiin (alligator)

Minoan Pottery #1

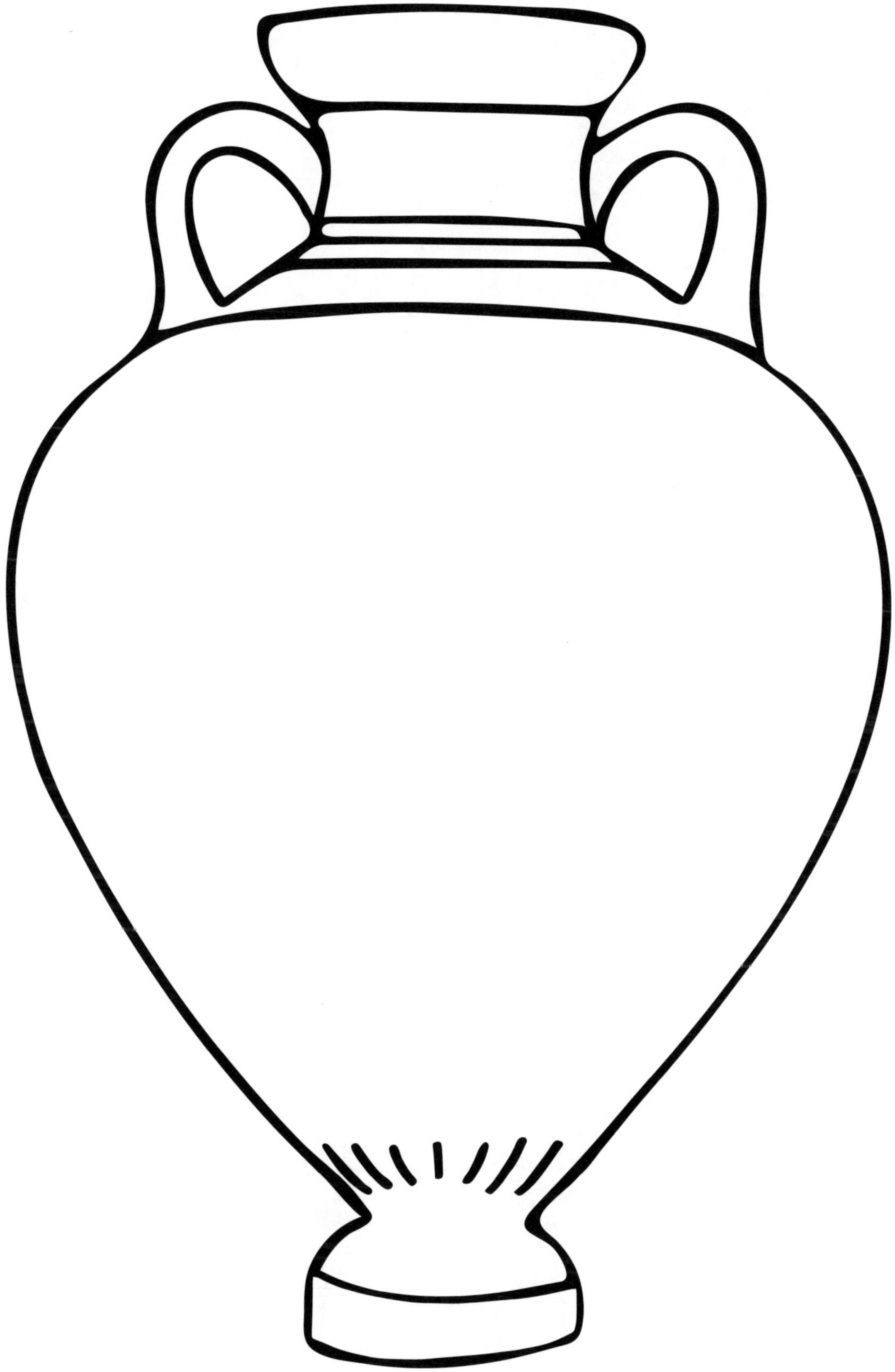

Minoan Pottery #2

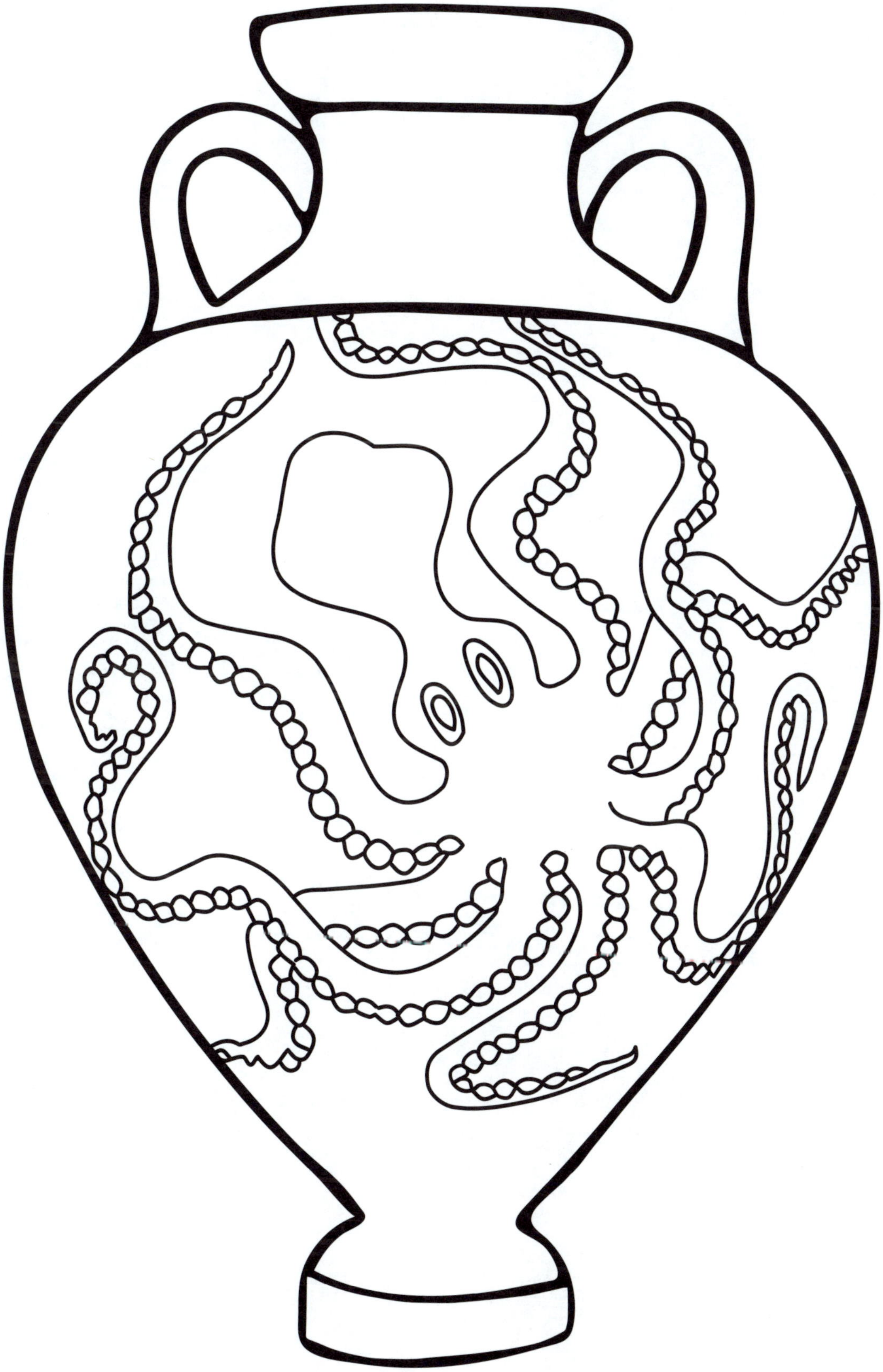

Polyphemus

Roman Numerals

Numerals 1 to 12

I	II	III	IV	V	VI
1	2	3	4	5	6

VII	VIII	IX	X	XI	XII
7	8	9	10	11	12

Roman Numeral Symbols